A SHABBAT HAGGADAH

FOR CELEBRATION AND STUDY

Compiled by

MICHAEL STRASSFELD
Coeditor of the Jewish Catalog

INSTITUTE OF HUMAN RELATIONS PRESS
OF THE AMERICAN JEWISH COMMITTEE

about the author

MICHAEL STRASSFELD, researcher and writer, is best known as the coeditor of *The First Jewish Catalog* (1973), *The Second Jewish Catalog* (1976) and the forthcoming *Third Jewish Catalog* (1980). He is also the editor of the Rabbinical Assembly's *Passover Haggadah*.

Mr. Strassfeld is a founder of Minyan Mi'at in New York City and a former member of Havurat Shalom in Somerville, Mass. He was chairperson of the first National Havurah Conference in 1979, and has designed many innovative programs for Jewish education and communal involvement.

contents

foreword

This book is a tribute to Mordecai Kaplan, rabbi, Jewish philosopher and activist. It was he who, in the early 1970's, urged me to see that a "Shabbat Haggadah" be prepared and published. Dr. Kaplan was convinced that such a work was needed for Jews who were ambivalent about their Jewishness and unskilled in the customs and rituals of their tradition. And he believed such a publication should come from the American Jewish Committee, as a K'lal Yisrael organization, hospitable to diverse religious, cultural and political views.

Jewish life in America, more than ever, shows conflicting trends. There is much reason for concern about the Jewish future, much evidence of eroding Jewish identity; but there is also much promising ferment and change. Many Jews are seriously searching for the meaning of their Jewishness and for ways to express it; many more might do so, but lack sufficient motivation or knowledge.

Studies by the American Jewish Committee have found that adherence to Jewish values and active practice of Judaism are strongly correlated with a rich, well-functioning family life. Many of the problems families face today stem from lack of guiding beliefs and values, rather than of practical services and facilities.

To help remedy this lack, to strengthen the Jewish family by imbuing it with Jewish lore and spirit, is the American Jewish Committee's chief purpose in publishing the Shabbat Haggadah. The Committee has long been studying the Jewish family's needs and developing programs to help sustain and support it. In the fall of 1980, these efforts culminated in the creation of the National Jewish Family Center. This volume is one of the Center's first publications.

We hope that the Shabbat Haggadah will help make Jewish family life joyous and meaningful. Like the Passover Haggadah, on which it is modeled, it is designed to give structure to a celebration that combines reading, study and discussion with fellowship, celebration, songs, special food and wine. By serving as the framework of a weekly "shabbat seder," it seeks to create, all the year round, a sense of celebration like that which Passover—now the most widely celebrated Jewish holiday—affords on ·a larger and more profound scale once a year.

The sanctity of every seventh day is the hub and heart of Jewish practice and celebration. The Shabbat represents the fullness of Judaism as a way of life. It reflects Jewish belief, history and tradition, Jewish ethical and social ideas and ideals. The Rabbis taught that practicing Jews receive an extra "Shabbat soul," and that Shabbat is a foretaste of the messianic age, in which there will be no more emptiness, alienation or confusion.

We believe that, in our troubled times, there are many Jews who will find comfort and peace in the celebration of Shabbat on Friday evenings in their homes with family and friends. It is our hope that the *Shabbat Haggadah* will serve them as an introduction and guide to a joyous Jewish living experience.

The *Shabbat Haggadah* has been tested by some family groups and individuals but, being a first attempt of its kind, it is still in a tentative stage. We would greatly appreciate the comments and suggestions of all who use it. With the help of these reactions, we hope to modify and refine the book in future editions, so as to meet the needs of users as fully as possible.

Dr. Gladys Rosen, Program Specialist in the American Jewish Committee's Jewish Communal Affairs Department, has worked closely with the editor, Michael Strassfeld. We are also grateful to Dr. Barry Holtz and Dr. Paula Hyman, who served as advisors to the editor. Special thanks are due to Sonya F. Kaufer, AJC's Director of Publications, and to George Salomon, Senior Editor in the Publications Service, for their help in the preparation of this volume.

YEHUDA ROSENMAN
Coordinator, National Jewish Family Center
The American Jewish Committee

introduction

Shabbat is perhaps the most central institution in Judaism. Through it, we can bring ourselves to a new sense of family, of community, of peace. This book is patterned after the Passover Haggadah and designed to make the entry into Shabbat a little easier, by describing the Friday night observances and explaining how to perform them. Like the Passover Haggadah, it transforms a meal into a ritual.

The text is a mixture of prayer, story, song, and of study, integrating the concept of Talmud Torah—the study of Jewish texts—into the traditional Shabbat celebration. The twelve units of study presented here consist of texts with commentary and questions for discussion.

We have chosen this format because the ability to study and confront Jewish texts is fundamental to being a Jew. We believe that Jews, who have always revered the word—revered it enough to study it, challenge it and be challenged by it—must not allow themselves to lose the ability merely because of language difficulties. Our conviction is that such study is open to anyone, regardless of the depth or shallowness of his or her Jewish background; our hope is that if we only point the way, people will be able to rediscover the joy of serious study.

The texts chosen represent the full range and variety of Jewish literature over the last three thousand years—from the Biblical to the contemporary, from legal writings to fanciful fables. Perhaps more important, they serve as illustrations of fundamental Jewish themes—God, prayer, redemption, *tzedaka* (charity), law, etc.

You should not be intimidated by these texts, nor should you look to this book for answers to the questions they raise. The selections, while short, have a multiplicity of answers and are open to interpretation at many levels. It is your interaction with the text, perhaps even your disagreement with it, that is crucial. The goal is not to arrive at some conclusion—the end—as we do in reading a novel. It is to realize that we can never reach a conclusion—that we may have learned something about Judaism and perhaps about ourselves, but that the process is, by its very nature, never concluded.

Our hope, then, is that by combining the ritual of Shabbat with the experience of study we will enhance not only the two experiences, but our lives as well.

How to Use the Haggadah

Part I, "Erev Shabbat Celebration and Ritual," explains the various Friday night rituals. Families or groups which have their own traditions for Shabbat observance will probably want to use this material selectively. Others just getting acquainted with Shabbat, or interested in experimenting with new practices, may want to perform most or all of the rituals included. This material, then, is presented as a resource, not as a prescription, for Shabbat observance.

Part II, "Shabbat Study Texts," is the heart of this book. It can be dealt with in different ways, depending upon the size, composition and age of the group or family. Some suggestions follow:

1. The twelve units of the Haggadah can be taken at whatever pace the group or family sets for itself, monthly or at weekly study sessions. The texts are arranged in an order that is partly chronological, beginning with the meaning of Shabbat, since that is the focus of this publication, and ending with redemption, modernity and Israel. We have tried to vary the types of texts. You should feel free to change the order or even skip a text.

2. It is a good idea to have one member of the family or group look over the text in advance to decide how to present it and which questions or issues to raise and examine. This person can also help direct the discussion, keep people focused on the important questions, and decide when to continue with study and when to end the evening. While some groups may want to dispense with a formal discussion leader, it is still important for someone to become familiar with the text *before* the group meeting.

3. *To the discussion leader:* Make sure that everyone understands what is being said. All concepts should be explained and all Hebrew terms translated. Try to involve everyone in the discussion and not to let two or three people monopolize the conversation.

Be aware of the attention span of the group. Even if a small number (including yourself) is still involved in a heated discussion, the majority may be tired or bored. If the specific question is not interesting to the others, move on to the next. If the group has grappled with the text and exhausted it, it is best to end the formal part of the evening, leaving it to individuals to continue the discussion on their own.

It is important to have a general sense of how long you (and the group) want the studying to last. Half an hour? An hour? More? Be flexible. If a good discussion is taking place, let it continue past your deadline. If the text has been fully discussed, do not prolong the evening just because at previous sessions the discussion went on longer.

4. Different types of texts should be handled differently. How this might be done is usually indicated in the introduction to the text, but some general suggestions follow.

For story texts:

a. Read the material through once, either out loud or silently. If it is long, silent reading might be preferable.

b. Look at the questions—particularly the general questions. You may want to have a short preliminary discussion on the problems the story confronts.

c. Reread the story more carefully out loud and then begin the discussion. If the story is long, you may want to allow for short comments as it is read.

For legal or other nonfiction texts:

a. Each section should be read and discussed individually.

b. Sometimes it may be useful to compare the sections in an attempt to gain an overview of the issue—for example in Unit VIII on the value of life.

5. The questions are to help initiate discussion. Usually there are more questions than any group or family can answer. Some may want to skip the questions altogether and rely on their own reading of the text. Others may want to focus solely on the general questions. In no event should it be felt that all questions must be answered; indeed, it is our hope that your group will raise questions not even presented here.

6. *Concerning children*: We are faced with a dilemma: how to include texts that will be exciting to both children and adults. The levels range from the apparently simple to the complex. We hope most of the texts will prove appropriate for a variety of age levels. However, if children are present, it is

crucial to review the texts ahead of time, before discussing them with the children. Only you know the intellectual sophistication of your children and can decide which texts can be presented to them.

With each text, we have tried to provide some questions especially suitable for children. In general, depending on the age of the children, you may want to:

a. Explain the text more fully beforehand and as you read it.
b. Retell the story or text in simpler language.
c. Have the children (especially if they are very young) play together in another room while the rest of the family discusses the text. This activity should be structured so that the children have something constructive to do that will prevent your discussion from being constantly interrupted. A variant on this practice is to have the children there for the text or story and carry on an initial discussion with them based on the questions for children, after which they leave and the adults continue the discussion on a different level. In this way, the children quickly come to realize that such study is important to you, and that you want them to participate when possible. Still another way to involve young children is by teaching them a song or a part of the Friday night ritual. Thus, even if children do not participate in study, they will know that Shabbat is special.

7. For those who wish to explore further the meaning of Shabbat or study additional texts, we have provided a bibliography. We have also included a list of cassettes and records of traditional and folk melodies for Friday night.

8. Do not let the discussion lose sight of the main question or theme of the text. While details matter, the texts were chosen because of the fundamental importance of their themes. It is also essential to make people relate personally to the text, not just discuss it academically. The purpose of study is to grapple with texts and connect them to our lives and experiences, not just to discover their abstract meaning.

A final note: You should not feel that every text must be totally understood. Some contain paradoxes which, by their very nature, cannot be explained. Their point is to raise and perhaps clarify issues, rather than to answer questions definitively. We recommend that you purchase a loose-leaf notebook or binder in which to collect articles, stories, poems, etc., to complement the present material or to be used for additional study texts.

PART I

Erev Shabbat
Celebration and Ritual

$\mathcal{S}$habbat is a day so precious, so extraordinary, that to write about it seems an almost superhuman task—or perhaps a sacrilege. How can one explain a period of timelessness set off from the week, when our frenetically moving activities slowly come to a halt and a sense of unutterable peace, soul-calm and tranquility can begin to be felt?

Shabbat originated at the beginning of time. The Bible (Genesis 2:2-3) says: "On the seventh day God finished the work which He had been doing, and He rested on the seventh day from all the work which He had done. And God blessed the seventh day and declared it holy, because on it God ceased from all the work of creation which He had done."

Shabbat, then, is the climax to the six days of creation. Why should this be so? Why was it necessary for God to rest on the seventh day? God's resting is to serve as an example to us of how we should live. Thus, the first week of creation, with its six days of work followed by Shabbat, becomes the pattern for each succeeding week.

It is stated in the Ten Commandments (Exodus 20:9-10): "Six days you shall labor and do all your work, but the seventh day is a sabbath of the Lord your God." The Jewish tradition views work as an act with intrinsic value and meaning, not just a necessity of living. Therefore, for six days each week we are partners with God in the ongoing creation of the world. Shabbat, however, calls a halt to that process of creativity. This rest is to enable us to gain a perspective on our work. In fact, refraining from work on Shabbat is what allows us to be creative during the rest of the week. Without it, work would become drudgery; without it we would once again become slaves to Pharaoh in Egypt, constantly occupied in our lives with building pyramids which are monuments to death, not life.

This is not to deny that Shabbat is also for physical rest. It is a day for an afternoon nap and for long and leisurely meals. Indeed, the institution of Shabbat was revolutionary in calling for a halt to ceaseless work; yet the role of Shabbat as a physical rest is less important than its function as a spiritual rest.

Shabbat is created by refraining from *melakhah*—work—and by trying to establish a state of *menuchah*—rest and repose. It is a unique kind of

9

rest—a special kind of tranquility, different from the relaxation of a vacation. As Erich Fromm writes:

> Rest in the sense of the traditional Sabbath is quite different from "rest" being defined as not working, or not making an effort (just as "peace"— shalom—in the prophetic tradition is more than merely the absence of war; it expresses harmony, wholeness). On the Sabbath, man ceases completely to be an animal whose main occupation is to fight for survival and to sustain his biological life. On the Sabbath, man is fully man, with no task other than to be human.[1]

It is, as Abraham Joshua Heschel has written,

> . . . not a day of frivolity but to mend our tattered lives, to collect rather than dissipate them.
>
> Shabbat is not renouncing of technical civilization, just an attempt to gain some independence of it.
>
> For six days a week, we seek to dominate the world; on the seventh, we try to dominate the self.[2]

Throughout Jewish history, Shabbat has been seen as a precious gift from God to the Jewish people. No matter how poor a Jew was, or how persecuted and despised by the surrounding world, on Shabbat he entered another world, a world of joy, of festive eating, of freedom from weekday tribulations. On Shabbat, each Jew becomes a king or queen, each home becomes a palace. Shabbat is said to be *me'ein olam haba*—a taste of the world to come, a time of peace and harmony. Ahad Ha'am, the noted Zionist philosopher, stated that, more than the Jews have observed Shabbat, Shabbat has preserved the Jews.[3]

This period from twilight on Friday to Saturday evening gives us the opportunity to begin to let ourselves feel intense love and joy and appreciate that which we are often too busy to notice during the week. We can let our emotions come out—acknowledge them, know them so intensely that each moment becomes a complete experience. It is a time to be with family and friends, a time to re-examine the past week before plunging into the new one.

Hakhanah le-Shabbat—Preparation for Shabbat

The days in the Jewish calendar have no names equivalent to Sunday, Monday, etc. Rather, they are counted: "the first day to Shabbat," "the second day to Shabbat," and so on. Only Shabbat, the seventh day, is called by a name, for it is the climax of the whole week. Directing the week toward Shabbat in this way affects not only the calendar but the orientation of our lives. There is a tradition, for example, of putting aside one's best clothes or a choice food for Shabbat. This week-long preparation intensifies, the closer we get to Shabbat.

On Friday (*erev shabbat*) we ready ourselves both physically and mentally for Shabbat. The house is cleaned and food is prepared. Toward evening, we shower and put on fresh clothes—and begin to unwind. Slowly, we open ourselves to the newness of another Shabbat—the rediscovery of places within ourselves that remain unexplored during the hectic activity of the week.

To foster anticipation and appreciation of Shabbat, it is best to try to include everyone in the preparations. Whether by cleaning one's room, or by setting or decorating the Shabbat table, everyone should take notice that Shabbat is approaching. There should be a feeling that Shabbat is different—because of dress, a special white tablecloth, or the Shabbat candles that are placed on or near the table.

Kabbalat Shabbat—Friday Night

The Friday night service is called *kabbalat shabbat*, which means "welcoming (or receiving) the Shabbat." The mood of this service, and of the evening as well, is one of rejoicing and of harmony—a time of quiet celebration with family or friends. It reflects the imagery of the service: the Shabbat as the bride of the people of Israel.

> The symbol of a bride is love, devotion, and joy—an inward feeling. It is the peculiar inward feeling of the Jew which characterizes the Sabbath day. To him the Sabbath is a bride. Just as one prepares for a bride with the utmost care and meticulous detail, so the Sabbath is preceded by careful preparation. Just as one yearns for the arrival of a bride, so is the Sabbath met and welcomed. Just as the presence of the bride elicits tender concern, so does the Sabbath evoke love and devotion. Just as the departure of a bride occasions sadness, so is the departure of the Sabbath in darkness and regret.[4]

Hadlakat Neirot—Lighting Candles

It is customary for the woman in the household to light at least two Shabbat candles on Friday evening. (Some people light more than the minimum two; for example, one for each member of the family.) The traditional two candles represent the two versions of the injunction concerning Shabbat found in the Ten Commandments:

Remember (*zakhor*) the Sabbath day to keep it holy (Exodus 20:8).

Observe (*shamor*) the Sabbath day to keep it holy (Deuteronomy 5:12).

These Shabbat lights have a dual symbolism:

1. Since Shabbat is a day of joy and pleasure (*oneg shabbat*), we begin the day by bringing into our homes the symbol of that joy—light.
2. Since Shabbat is a day of peace (*shalom*), we introduce harmony in the home (*shalom bayit*) by lighting candles which will illuminate our Friday night meal. (For this reason, the candles should be lit on or near the table in the dining room.)

Customarily the candles are lit before sunset. Thus they become a symbol of all the preparations made so as not to violate the prohibition against working on Shabbat. Since one of these commandments prohibits creating light, many people are careful to light the candles approximately twenty minutes or more before sunset. Others, however, follow the custom of lighting the candles right before the meal.

After lighting the candles, many individuals cover their eyes and then recite the blessing. Others draw their hands around the candles and toward their faces, symbolically drawing the light of the candles into themselves and their homes. The reason for these two customs (often people observe both) is a little complicated. A blessing is usually recited before an act. However, since the blessing over the Shabbat candles is seen by some as initiating Shabbat, it would be forbidden to light a fire after the blessing is said. To get around this problem, the candles are lit, and then you cover your eyes while the blessing is recited. Since your eyes are covered, it is as though the candles are not yet lit. Thus, when you open your eyes, the already lit candles can be enjoyed for the first time, and you complete the blessing without violating Shabbat. Others simply say the blessing and light the candles, considering both together as the initiation of Shabbat.

Candles should be lit in every home. Accordingly, while it is customary for women to light the candles, men may light them as well.

בָּרוּךְ אַתָּה, יְיָ אֱלֹהֵינוּ, מֶלֶךְ הָעוֹלָם, אֲשֶׁר קִדְּשָׁנוּ בְּמִצְוֹתָיו וְצִוָּנוּ לְהַדְלִיק נֵר שֶׁל שַׁבָּת.

Barukh attah Adonai eloheinu melekh ha-olam asher kidshanu be-mitzvotav ve-tzivanu le-hadlik neir shel shabbat.

Praised are You, Lord our God, King of the Universe who has sanctified our lives through His commandments, commanding us to kindle the Sabbath lights.

Finally, many add prayers of their choice after the candle lighting. One example of such a traditional prayer:

PRAYER OF A JEWISH WOMAN BEFORE LIGHTING THE CANDLES

O God of Your people Israel:
You are holy
And you have made the Sabbath and the people of Israel holy.
You have called upon us to honor the Sabbath with light,
With joy
And with peace—
As a king and queen give love to one another;
So have we kindled these two lights for love of your daughter,
The Sabbath day.

Almighty God.
Grant me and all my loved ones
A choice to truly rest on this Sabbath day.
May the light of the candles drive out from among us
The spirit of anger, the spirit of harm.
Send your blessings to my children,
That they may walk in the ways of Your Torah, Your light.
May You ever be their God
And mine, O Lord,
My Creator and my Redeemer.
Amen.[5]

Shalom Aleikhem—Peace Be Unto You

We welcome the Sabbath by singing this hymn welcoming the angels of peace.

שָׁלוֹם עֲלֵיכֶם. מַלְאֲכֵי הַשָּׁרֵת. מַלְאֲכֵי עֶלְיוֹן.
מִמֶּלֶךְ מַלְכֵי הַמְּלָכִים. הַקָּדוֹשׁ בָּרוּךְ הוּא.

13

בוֹאֲכֶם לְשָׁלוֹם. מַלְאֲכֵי הַשָּׁלוֹם, מַלְאֲכֵי עֶלְיוֹן.
מִמֶּלֶךְ מַלְכֵי הַמְּלָכִים, הַקָּדוֹשׁ בָּרוּךְ הוּא.

בָּרְכוּנִי לְשָׁלוֹם. מַלְאֲכֵי הַשָּׁלוֹם. מַלְאֲכֵי עֶלְיוֹן.
מִמֶּלֶךְ מַלְכֵי הַמְּלָכִים. הַקָּדוֹשׁ בָּרוּךְ הוּא.

צֵאתְכֶם לְשָׁלוֹם. מַלְאֲכֵי הַשָּׁלוֹם. מַלְאֲכֵי עֶלְיוֹן.
מִמֶּלֶךְ מַלְכֵי הַמְּלָכִים, הַקָּדוֹשׁ בָּרוּךְ הוּא.

Shalom aleikhem, mal'akhei ha-shareit mal'akhei elyon,
Mimelekh mal'khei ha-m'lakhim ha-kadosh barukh hu.

Boakhem le-shalom mal'akhei . . .

Barkhuni le-shalom mal'akhei . . .

Tzeitkhem le-shalom mal'akhei . . .

Peace be unto you, ministering angels, angels of the most High,
The Supreme King of Kings, The Holy One, blessed be He.

Enter in peace, angels of peace . . .

Bless me with peace . . .

Depart in peace . . .

Personal Blessings

We continue trying to bring *shalom bayit,* peace and harmony, into our
homes by blessing those gathered together this evening. On the following
pages there are blessings and praise of children, the wife and the husband.
Those gathered with friends or in a group might like to bless each other by
reciting the priestly blessing. Some do this by placing a hand on the heads
of each of the people next to them while reciting together the following
(Numbers 6:24-26):

יְבָרֶכְךָ יְיָ וְיִשְׁמְרֶךָ.
יָאֵר יְיָ פָּנָיו אֵלֶיךָ וִיחֻנֶּךָּ.
יִשָּׂא יְיָ פָּנָיו אֵלֶיךָ וְיָשֵׂם לְךָ שָׁלוֹם.

Yevarekhekha Adonai ve-yishmerekha
Ya-eir Adonai panav eilekha vi-chuneka
Yisa Adonai panav eilekha ve-yaseim lekha shalom.

May the Lord bless you and keep you.
May the Lord deal kindly and graciously with you.
May the Lord bestow His favor upon you, and grant you peace.

Blessing the Children

It is customary for parents to bless their children before the meal. Place both hands upon your child's head and recite:

For a girl:

יְשִׂימֵךְ אֱלֹהִים כְּשָׂרָה. רִבְקָה. רָחֵל. וְלֵאָה.

Ye'simeikh elohim ke-sarah, rivkah, racheil, ve-le'ah.

May God make you as Sarah, Rebecca, Rachel and Leah.

For a boy (Genesis 48:20):

יְשִׂימְךָ אֱלֹהִים כְּאֶפְרַיִם וְכִמְנַשֶּׁה.

Ye'simkha elohim ke-ephrayim ve-khi-menasheh.

May God make you as Ephraim and Menasheh.

15

Continue with the priestly blessing (Numbers 6:24-26):

יְבָרֶכְךָ יְיָ וְיִשְׁמְרֶךָ.
יָאֵר יְיָ פָּנָיו אֵלֶיךָ וִיחֻנֶּךָּ.
יִשָּׂא יְיָ פָּנָיו אֵלֶיךָ וְיָשֵׂם לְךָ שָׁלוֹם.

Yevarakhekha Adonai ve-yishmerekha
Ya-eir Adonai panav eilekha vi-chuneka
Yisa Adonai panav eilekha ve-yaseim lekha shalom.

May the Lord bless you and keep you.
May the Lord deal kindly and graciously with you.
May the Lord bestow His favor upon you, and grant you peace.

Eishet Chayil—A Woman of Valor

Eishet Chayil, taken from the Book of Proverbs (31:10-31), is a hymn of praise traditionally sung by the husband to honor the wife:

אֵשֶׁת חַיִל מִי יִמְצָא   וְרָחֹק מִפְּנִינִים מִכְרָהּ.
בָּטַח בָּהּ לֵב בַּעְלָהּ   וְשָׁלָל לֹא יֶחְסָר.
גְּמָלַתְהוּ טוֹב וְלֹא רָע   כֹּל יְמֵי חַיֶּיהָ.
דָּרְשָׁה צֶמֶר וּפִשְׁתִּים   וַתַּעַשׂ בְּחֵפֶץ כַּפֶּיהָ.
הָיְתָה כָּאֳנִיּוֹת סוֹחֵר   מִמֶּרְחָק תָּבִיא לַחְמָהּ.
וַתָּקָם בְּעוֹד לַיְלָה   וַתִּתֵּן טֶרֶף לְבֵיתָהּ וְחֹק לְנַעֲרֹתֶיהָ.
זָמְמָה שָׂדֶה וַתִּקָּחֵהוּ   מִפְּרִי כַפֶּיהָ נָטְעָה כָּרֶם.
חָגְרָה בְעוֹז מָתְנֶיהָ   וַתְּאַמֵּץ זְרוֹעֹתֶיהָ.
טָעֲמָה כִּי טוֹב סַחְרָהּ   לֹא יִכְבֶּה בַלַּיְלָה נֵרָהּ.
יָדֶיהָ שִׁלְּחָה בַכִּישׁוֹר   וְכַפֶּיהָ תָּמְכוּ פָלֶךְ.
כַּפָּהּ פָּרְשָׂה לֶעָנִי   וְיָדֶיהָ שִׁלְּחָה לָאֶבְיוֹן.
לֹא תִירָא לְבֵיתָהּ מִשָּׁלֶג   כִּי כָל בֵּיתָהּ לָבֻשׁ שָׁנִים.

מַרְבַדִּים עָשְׂתָה לָּהּ   שֵׁשׁ וְאַרְגָּמָן לְבוּשָׁהּ.

נוֹדָע בַּשְּׁעָרִים בַּעְלָהּ   בְּשִׁבְתּוֹ עִם זִקְנֵי אָרֶץ.

סָדִין עָשְׂתָה וַתִּמְכֹּר   וַחֲגוֹר נָתְנָה לַכְּנַעֲנִי.

עֹז וְהָדָר לְבוּשָׁהּ   וַתִּשְׂחַק לְיוֹם אַחֲרוֹן.

פִּיהָ פָּתְחָה בְחָכְמָה   וְתוֹרַת חֶסֶד עַל לְשׁוֹנָהּ.

צוֹפִיָּה הֲלִיכוֹת בֵּיתָהּ   וְלֶחֶם עַצְלוּת לֹא תֹאכֵל.

קָמוּ בָנֶיהָ וַיְאַשְּׁרוּהָ   בַּעְלָהּ וַיְהַלְלָהּ.

רַבּוֹת בָּנוֹת עָשׂוּ חָיִל   וְאַתְּ עָלִית עַל כֻּלָּנָה.

שֶׁקֶר הַחֵן וְהֶבֶל הַיֹּפִי   אִשָּׁה יִרְאַת יְיָ הִיא תִתְהַלָּל.

תְּנוּ לָהּ מִפְּרִי יָדֶיהָ   וִיהַלְלוּהָ בַשְּׁעָרִים מַעֲשֶׂיהָ.

Chorus:
Eishet chayil mi yimtza?
v'rachok mi-p'ninim mikhra.

A woman of valor who can find?
For her price is far above rubies.
The heart of her husband does safely trust in her,
And he has no lack of gain.
She does him good and not evil
All the days of her life.
She seeks wool and flax,
And works willingly with her hands.
She is like the merchant-ships;
She brings her food from afar.
She rises also while it is yet night,
And gives food to her household,
And a portion to her maidens.

She considers a field, and buys it;
With the fruit of her hands she plants a vineyard.
She girds her loins with strength,
And makes strong her arms.
She perceives that her merchandise is good;
Her lamp goes not out by night.
She lays her hands to the distaff,
And her hands hold the spindle.

She stretches out her hand to the poor;
Yea, she reaches forth her hands to the needy.

She is not afraid of the snow for her household;
For all her household are clothed with scarlet.
She makes for herself coverlets;
Her clothing is fine linen and purple.
Her husband is known in the gates,
When he sits among the elders of the land.
She makes linen garments and sells them;
And delivers girdles unto the merchant.
Strength and dignity are her clothing;
And she laughs at the time to come.
She opens her mouth with wisdom;
And the law of kindness is on her tongue.

She looks well to the ways of her household,
And eats not the bread of idleness.
Her children rise up, and call her blessed;
Her husband also, and he praises her;
Many daughters have done valiantly,
But you excel them all.
Grace is deceitful, and beauty is vain;
But a woman that fears the Lord, she shall be praised.
Give her of the fruit of her hands;
And let her works praise her in the gates.

Blessed is the Man

For those who would like an analogous selection in praise of the husband,
we include a suggested reading (Psalms 112):

הַלְלוּ־יָהּ

אַשְׁרֵי־אִישׁ יָרֵא אֶת־יְיָ   בְּמִצְוֹתָיו חָפֵץ מְאֹד:

גִּבּוֹר בָּאָרֶץ יִהְיֶה זַרְעוֹ   דּוֹר יְשָׁרִים יְבֹרָךְ:

הוֹן־וָעֹשֶׁר בְּבֵיתוֹ   וְצִדְקָתוֹ עֹמֶדֶת לָעַד:

זָרַח בַּחֹשֶׁךְ אוֹר לַיְשָׁרִים   חַנּוּן וְרַחוּם וְצַדִּיק:

מִשְׁמוּעָה רָעָה לֹא יִירָא   נָכוֹן לִבּוֹ בָּטֻחַ בַּיְיָ:
סָמוּךְ לִבּוֹ לֹא יִירָא   פִּזַּר נָתַן לָאֶבְיוֹנִים
צִדְקָתוֹ עֹמֶדֶת לָעַד   קַרְנוֹ תָּרוּם בְּכָבוֹד:

Blessed is the man who reveres the Lord,
Who greatly delights in God's commandments!
His descendants will be honored in the land:
The generation of the upright will be blessed.
His household prospers,
And his righteousness endures forever.
Light dawns in the darkness for the upright;
For the one who is gracious, compassionate, and just.
He is not afraid of evil tidings;
His mind is firm, trusting in the Lord.
His heart is steady, he will not be afraid.
He has distributed freely, he has given to the poor;
His righteousness endures forever;
His life is exalted in honor.

Alternatively, the husband and wife may like to recite to each other the following verses from *Shir ha-Shirim*—the Song of Songs (2:16; 8:6–7; 6:3; 4:9–10; 2:10–13):

דּוֹדִי לִי וַאֲנִי לוֹ הָרֹעֶה בַּשּׁוֹשַׁנִּים:
שִׂימֵנִי כַחוֹתָם עַל־לִבֶּךָ כַּחוֹתָם עַל־זְרוֹעֶךָ
כִּי־עַזָּה כַמָּוֶת אַהֲבָה קָשָׁה כִשְׁאוֹל
קִנְאָה רְשָׁפֶיהָ רִשְׁפֵּי אֵשׁ שַׁלְהֶבֶתְיָה:
מַיִם רַבִּים לֹא יוּכְלוּ לְכַבּוֹת אֶת־הָאַהֲבָה וּנְהָרוֹת לֹא יִשְׁטְפוּהָ
אִם־יִתֵּן אִישׁ אֶת־כָּל־הוֹן בֵּיתוֹ בָּאַהֲבָה בּוֹז יָבוּזוּ לוֹ:

Dodi li va'ani lo, ha-roeh ba-shoshanim.

Woman:

My beloved is mine and I am his who browses among the lilies.
Let me be a seal upon your heart, like the seal upon your hand,
For love is fierce as death, passion is mighty as Sheol;

Its darts are darts of fire, a blazing flame.
Vast floods cannot quench love, nor rivers drown it.
If a man offered all his wealth for love, he would be laughed to
scorn.

אֲנִי לְדוֹדִי וְדוֹדִי לִי הָרוֹעֶה בַּשּׁוֹשַׁנִּים:

לִבַּבְתִּנִי אֲחֹתִי כַלָּה

לִבַּבְתִּנִי בְּאַחַת מֵעֵינַיִךְ בְּאַחַד עֲנָק מִצַּוְּרֹנָיִךְ:

מַה־יָּפוּ דֹדַיִךְ אֲחֹתִי כַלָּה מַה־טֹּבוּ דֹדַיִךְ מִיַּיִן

וְרֵיחַ שְׁמָנַיִךְ מִכָּל־בְּשָׂמִים:

Man:

I am my beloved's and my beloved is mine.
You have captured my heart, my own, my bride,
You have captured my heart, with one glance of your eyes,
With one coil of your necklace.
How sweet is your love, my own, my bride!
How much more delightful your love than wine,
Your ointments more fragrant than any spice!

עָנָה דוֹדִי וְאָמַר לִי קוּמִי לָךְ רַעְיָתִי יָפָתִי וּלְכִי־לָךְ:

כִּי־הִנֵּה הַסְּתָו עָבָר הַגֶּשֶׁם חָלַף הָלַךְ לוֹ:

הַנִּצָּנִים נִרְאוּ בָאָרֶץ עֵת הַזָּמִיר הִגִּיעַ

וְקוֹל הַתּוֹר נִשְׁמַע בְּאַרְצֵנוּ:

הַתְּאֵנָה חָנְטָה פַגֶּיהָ וְהַגְּפָנִים סְמָדַר נָתְנוּ רֵיחַ

קוּמִי לָךְ רַעְיָתִי יָפָתִי וּלְכִי־לָךְ:

Together:

My beloved spoke thus to me,
"Arise, my darling; my fair one, come away!
For now the winter is past, the rains are over and gone.
The blossoms have appeared in the land, the time of singing has
come;
The song of the turtledoves is heard in our land.
The green figs form on the fig trees, the vines in blossom give off
fragrance.
Arise, my darling; my fair one, come away!"

Kiddush—Sanctifying the Day

Kiddush is recited on the eve of every festival and Shabbat. It is customarily said over wine, a symbol of joy, as it is written, "wine gladdens the heart of man" (Psalms 104:15). Kiddush also reminds us that God gave us the power to sanctify time, to sanctify the Sabbath day.

Customs for the recital of Kiddush vary. Most people say it while standing, although some remain seated. The cup is lifted as Kiddush is recited.

וַיְהִי עֶרֶב וַיְהִי בְקֶר

יוֹם הַשִּׁשִּׁי. וַיְכֻלּוּ הַשָּׁמַיִם וְהָאָרֶץ וְכָל צְבָאָם. וַיְכַל אֱלֹהִים בַּיּוֹם הַשְּׁבִיעִי מְלַאכְתּוֹ אֲשֶׁר עָשָׂה, וַיִּשְׁבֹּת בַּיּוֹם הַשְּׁבִיעִי מִכָּל־מְלַאכְתּוֹ אֲשֶׁר עָשָׂה. וַיְבָרֶךְ אֱלֹהִים אֶת יוֹם הַשְּׁבִיעִי וַיְקַדֵּשׁ אֹתוֹ, כִּי בוֹ שָׁבַת מִכָּל־מְלַאכְתּוֹ אֲשֶׁר בָּרָא אֱלֹהִים לַעֲשׂוֹת.

בָּרוּךְ אַתָּה, יְיָ אֱלֹהֵינוּ, מֶלֶךְ הָעוֹלָם, בּוֹרֵא פְּרִי הַגָּפֶן.

בָּרוּךְ אַתָּה, יְיָ אֱלֹהֵינוּ, מֶלֶךְ הָעוֹלָם, אֲשֶׁר קִדְּשָׁנוּ בְּמִצְוֹתָיו וְרָצָה בָנוּ, וְשַׁבַּת קָדְשׁוֹ בְּאַהֲבָה וּבְרָצוֹן הִנְחִילָנוּ, זִכָּרוֹן לְמַעֲשֵׂה בְרֵאשִׁית. כִּי הוּא יוֹם תְּחִלָּה לְמִקְרָאֵי קֹדֶשׁ, זֵכֶר לִיצִיאַת מִצְרָיִם. כִּי־בָנוּ בָחַרְתָּ וְאוֹתָנוּ קִדַּשְׁתָּ מִכָּל־הָעַמִּים, וְשַׁבַּת קָדְשְׁךָ בְּאַהֲבָה וּבְרָצוֹן הִנְחַלְתָּנוּ. בָּרוּךְ אַתָּה, יְיָ, מְקַדֵּשׁ הַשַּׁבָּת.

There was evening and there was morning, the sixth day. The heavens and the earth, and all they contain, were completed. On the seventh day God finished the work which He had been doing; He ceased on the seventh day from all the work which He had done. Then God blessed the seventh day and called it holy, because on it He ceased from all His work of creation.

Praised are You, Lord our God, King of the Universe, who creates the fruit of the vine.

Praised are You, Lord our God, King of the Universe, who has sanctified us through His commandments and has been pleased with us. You have lovingly and gladly granted us Your holy Sabbath, recalling the creation of the world. The Sabbath is first among the days of sacred assembly which recall the Exodus from

Egypt. You have chosen us, sanctifying us among all people by granting us Your holy Sabbath lovingly and gladly. Praised are You, Lord, who sanctifies the Sabbath.

Netilat Yadayim—Washing

Some follow the custom of washing their hands before eating any meal, or at least before eating the Shabbat meals. Eating is seen as a holy act, and the Rabbis compare our tables to the altar in the Temple. Thus, we wash our hands, as did the priests, to sanctify the act of eating.

To perform the ritual washing, take a cup or pitcher of water in one hand and pour it over the other. Then reverse hands and do the same to your other hand. Some people do this three times on each hand. Recite the blessing and then dry your hands.

בָּרוּךְ אַתָּה, יְיָ אֱלֹהֵינוּ, מֶלֶךְ הָעוֹלָם,
אֲשֶׁר קִדְּשָׁנוּ בְּמִצְוֹתָיו וְצִוָּנוּ עַל נְטִילַת יָדֶיִם.

Barukh attah Adonai eloheinu melekh ha-olam
asher kidshanu be-mitzvotav ve-tzivanu al netilat yadayim.

Praised are You, Lord our God, King of the Universe,
who has sanctified us through His commandments, and
commanded us to wash our hands.

Some follow the custom of not talking between washing and eating, since washing is a preparation for the meal.

Motzi—Eating Bread

On Shabbat we use two loaves of bread called *challot* (singular *challah*), which recall the double portion of manna God caused to fall every Friday in the desert to provide for Shabbat, when no manna fell. It is customary before eating to take the *challot*, recite the blessing and then divide at least one loaf among the participants. Some observe the custom of salting the *challah* before eating, as another reminder of the Temple, in which salt was used during the sacrificial rites.

בָּרוּךְ אַתָּה, יְיָ אֱלֹהֵינוּ, מֶלֶךְ הָעוֹלָם,
הַמּוֹצִיא לֶחֶם מִן הָאָרֶץ.

Barukh attah Adonai eloheinu melekh ha-olam
ha-motzi lechem min ha-aretz.

Praised are You, Lord our God, King of the Universe,
who brings forth bread from the earth.

The Meal

The meal should be a time to enjoy one another's company, as well as to
celebrate Shabbat. As Eliezer Berkovits writes:

> The affirmation of earthly needs and vital impulses is characteristic of the
> whole system of the law of Judaism. Sabbath and holidays are not observed
> "spiritually," nor should they be so observed. Man is not a spirit. On the Sab-
> bath, therefore, not only the soul should find peace, but the body too should
> rest. One celebrates the day not only by meditation and prayer, but also by
> wearing Sabbath clothes and by partaking of the Sabbath meals. The Sab-
> bath meal itself is a mitzvah; it is a divine service. And if properly performed,
> it is a service of a far higher quality than that of prayer and meditation alone;
> it is the service of the whole man.

> The enjoyment of the Sabbath is neither spiritual nor material; it is wholly
> human. Body and spirit celebrate the Sabbath in communion. The Jew who
> keeps the Sabbath may say that the material enjoyments of the day enhance
> his spiritual elation and that his spiritual elation renders the material enjoy-
> ments more gratifying. In the unifying act of the mitzvah the Sabbath acts as
> "a spice" to the palate and as an exhilarating joy for the spirit of man.[6]

Zemirot—Songs

It is the custom to rejoice during the meal by singing songs in praise of
Shabbat and of God. A number of songs, many dating to the Middle Ages,
have become traditional; some of these appear here. However, you can also
sing other songs (in Hebrew or English) which are in the spirit of Shabbat.
Thus, we have are also included some modern Hebrew songs.

צוּר מִשֶּׁלוֹ

TZUR MI-SHELO

צוּר מִשֶּׁלוֹ אָכַלְנוּ. בָּרְכוּ אֱמוּנַי.
שָׂבַעְנוּ וְהוֹתַרְנוּ כִּדְבַר יְיָ:

23

הַזָּן אֶת עוֹלָמוֹ. רוֹעֵנוּ אָבִינוּ.
אָכַלְנוּ אֶת לַחְמוֹ וְיֵינוֹ שָׁתִינוּ.

עַל כֵּן נוֹדֶה לִשְׁמוֹ וּנְהַלְלוֹ בְּפִינוּ.
אָמַרְנוּ וְעָנִינוּ. אֵין קָדוֹשׁ כַּיְיָ: צוּר מִשֶּׁלוֹ ...

Tzur mi-shelo akhalnu barkhu emunai
Savanu ve-hotarnu ki-dvar Adonai.

Ha-zan et olamo ro'einu avinu
Akhalnu et lachmo ve-yeino shatinu

Al kein nodeh lishmo u-nehalelo be-finu
Amarnu ve-aninu ein kadosh k'Adonai.

Let us bless our Rock who sustains us;
Like a shepherd, our Father feeds the world,
We have eaten his bread and drunk His wine,
Let us now praise His name.

מְנוּחָה וְשִׂמְחָה

MENUKHAH VE-SIMKHAH

מְנוּחָה וְשִׂמְחָה אוֹר לַיְּהוּדִים.
יוֹם שַׁבָּתוֹן יוֹם מַחֲמַדִּים.
שׁוֹמְרָיו וְזוֹכְרָיו הֵמָּה מְעִידִים.
כִּי לְשִׁשָּׁה כֹּל בְּרוּאִים וְעוֹמְדִים:

שְׁמֵי שָׁמַיִם אֶרֶץ וְיַמִּים.
כָּל־צְבָא מָרוֹם גְּבוֹהִים וְרָמִים.
תַּנִּין וְאָדָם וְחַיַּת רְאֵמִים.
כִּי בְּיָהּ יְיָ צוּר עוֹלָמִים:

הוּא אֲשֶׁר דִּבֶּר לְעַם סְגֻלָּתוֹ.
שָׁמוֹר לְקַדְּשׁוֹ מִבֹּאוֹ עַד־צֵאתוֹ.

שַׁבַּת קֹדֶשׁ יוֹם חֶמְדָּתוֹ.
כִּי בוֹ שָׁבַת אֵל מִכָּל־מְלַאכְתּוֹ:

Menuchah ve-simchah or la-yehudim
Yom shabbaton yom machmadim
Shomrav ve-zokhrav heimah me'idim
Ki le-shishah kol beru'im ve-omdim.

Sh'mei shamayim eretz ve-yamim
Kol tzvah marom g'vohim ve-ramim
Tanin ve-adam ve-chayat r'eimim
Ki be-yah Adonai tzur olamim.

Hu asher dibeir le-am segulato
Shamor le-kadsho mi-bo'o ve-ad tzeito
Shabbat kodesh yom chemdato
Ki vo shavat mi-kol melakhto.

Rest and delight mark this day;
Holiness and joy are its way.

ADDITIONAL SHABBAT ZEMIROT

אֵלֶּה חָמְדָה לִבִּי
חוּסָה נָא וְאַל נָא תִּתְעַלֵּם.

Eileh chamda libi.
Chusah na v'al na titalem.

These [Commandments] have my heart desired.
Have mercy and do not hide from us.

לֹא יִשָּׂא גוֹי אֶל גוֹי חֶרֶב
לֹא יִלְמְדוּ עוֹד מִלְחָמָה.

Lo yisa goi el goi cherev
Lo yilmedu od milchamah.

Nation shall not lift sword against nation
Nor shall they know war any more.

אֶרֶץ זָבַת חָלָב, חָלָב וּדְבַשׁ.

Eretz zavat chalav, chalav u'devash.

Land flowing with milk and honey.

וּפָרַצְתָּ יָמָה וָקֵדְמָה, צָפוֹנָה וָנֶגְבָּה.

U'faratzta yama, ve'keidma, tzafona, v'negba.

And you shall spread out—west, east, north, and south.

וְקָרֵב פְּזוּרֵינוּ מִבֵּין הַגּוֹיִים
וּנְפוּצוֹתֵינוּ כַּנֵּס מִיַּרְכְּתֵי אָרֶץ.

V'kareiv pezureinu mibein hagoyim
U'nefutzoteinu kanes m'yark'tei aretz.

Ingather our exiles from among the nations and
our dispersed from the corners of the earth.

יִשְׂמְחוּ בְמַלְכוּתְךָ
שׁוֹמְרֵי שַׁבָּת וְקוֹרְאֵי עוֹנֶג שַׁבָּת.

Yismechu be-malchutcha
Shomrei Shabbat vekorei oneg Shabbat.

Those who rejoice in the Shabbat will be joyful
under your Kingship.

לְכָה דוֹדִי לִקְרַאת כַּלָּה, פְּנֵי שַׁבָּת נְקַבְּלָה.

Lekha dodi likrat kalah
Pnei Shabbat nekablah.

Come, my love, to greet the Shabbat Queen.

עוֹד יִשָּׁמַע בְּעָרֵי יְהוּדָה
וּבְחוּצוֹת יְרוּשָׁלַיִם
קוֹל שָׂשׂוֹן וְקוֹל שִׂמְחָה
קוֹל חָתָן וְקוֹל כַּלָּה.

Od yishama beharei Yehuda
Uvchutzot yerushalayim
Kol sason vekol simcha
Kol chatan vekol kalah.

And yet will be heard in the mountains of Judah
and in the open air of Jerusalem
The voice of gladness and joy,
the voice of the bride and groom.

הַלְלוּיָה הַלְלוּיָה בְּצִלְצְלֵי שָׁמַע
הַלְלוּיָה, הַלְלוּיָה בְּצִלְצְלֵי תְרוּעָה
כֹּל הַנְּשָׁמָה תְהַלֵּל יָהּ
הַלְלוּיָה, הַלְלוּיָה.

Halleluyah, halleluyah betziltzelei shama
Halleluyah, halleluyah betziltzelei tru'a
Kol hanshama tehaleil yah
Halleluyah, halleluyah.

Halleluyah with sounds of trumpets.
All souls will praise God, Halleluyah.

הָבָה נָשִׁירָה שִׁיר הַלְלוּיָה.

Hava nashira shir halleluyah.

Let us sing a song—Halleluyah.

Birkat ha-Mazon—Prayer After Meals

The meal is concluded with *birkat ha-mazon*—a series of blessings and phrases which praise God for His goodness, and specifically for providing us with the food that sustains our lives. There are a number of versions of *birkat ha-mazon*. We have provided a short form and the traditional one. You may choose to recite it in its entirety or you may follow the short form.

Traditional Version

בִּרְכַּת הַמָּזוֹן

שִׁיר הַמַּעֲלוֹת

שִׁיר הַמַּעֲלוֹת בְּשׁוּב יהוה אֶת־שִׁיבַת צִיּוֹן הָיִינוּ כְּחֹלְמִים. אָז יִמָּלֵא שְׂחוֹק פִּינוּ וּלְשׁוֹנֵנוּ רִנָּה. אָז יֹאמְרוּ בַגּוֹיִם הִגְדִּיל יהוה לַעֲשׂוֹת עִם אֵלֶּה. הִגְדִּיל יהוה לַעֲשׂוֹת עִמָּנוּ הָיִינוּ שְׂמֵחִים. שׁוּבָה יהוה אֶת־שְׁבִיתֵנוּ כַּאֲפִיקִים בַּנֶּגֶב. הַזֹּרְעִים בְּדִמְעָה בְּרִנָּה יִקְצֹרוּ. הָלוֹךְ יֵלֵךְ וּבָכֹה נֹשֵׂא מֶשֶׁךְ הַזָּרַע בֹּא יָבֹא בְרִנָּה נֹשֵׂא אֲלֻמֹּתָיו.

When three or more adults have eaten together, one of them formally invites the others to join in these blessings. (When ten or more are present add the words in parentheses.)

רַבּוֹתַי נְבָרֵךְ.

The others respond, and the leader repeats:

יְהִי שֵׁם יְיָ מְבֹרָךְ מֵעַתָּה וְעַד עוֹלָם.

The leader continues:

בִּרְשׁוּת רַבּוֹתַי, נְבָרֵךְ (אֱלֹהֵינוּ) שֶׁאָכַלְנוּ מִשֶּׁלּוֹ.

The others respond, and the leader repeats:

בָּרוּךְ (אֱלֹהֵינוּ) שֶׁאָכַלְנוּ מִשֶּׁלּוֹ וּבְטוּבוֹ חָיִינוּ.

Leader and others:

בָּרוּךְ הוּא וּבָרוּךְ שְׁמוֹ.

BLESSINGS AFTER THE MEAL

Shir Hama-alot

When the Lord brought our exiles back to Zion, it was like a dream. Then our mouths were filled with laughter, joyous song was on our tongues. Then it was said among the nations: "The Lord has done great things for them." Great things indeed He did for us; therefore we rejoiced. Bring us back, O Lord, as You bring streams back to Israel's desert soil. Those who sow in tears shall reap with joyous song. A hungry man will plant in sadness, bearing his few sacks of seed; but he will come back home in gladness, bearing ample sheaves of grain.

When three or more adults have eaten together, one of them formally invites the others to join in these blessings. (When ten or more are present add the words in parentheses.)

Rabotai n'varekh.

Friends, let us give thanks.

The others respond, and the leader repeats:

Yehi shem Adonai mevorakh mei-attah v'ad olam.

May Adonai be praised, now and forever.

The leader continues:

Bir'shut rabotai, n'varekh (elo-heinu) sheh-akhalnu mi-shelo.

With your consent, friends, let us praise (our God) the One of whose food we have partaken.

The others respond, and the leader repeats:

Barukh (elo-heinu) sheh-akhalnu mi-shelo uve-tuvo chayinu.

Praised be (our God) the One of whose food we have partaken and by whose goodness we live.

Leader and others:

Barukh hu u-varukh sh'mo.

Praised be He and praised be His name.

בָּרוּךְ אַתָּה יְיָ אֱלֹהֵינוּ מֶלֶךְ הָעוֹלָם, הַזָּן אֶת־הָעוֹלָם כֻּלּוֹ בְּטוּבוֹ, בְּחֵן בְּחֶסֶד וּבְרַחֲמִים. הוּא נוֹתֵן לֶחֶם לְכָל־בָּשָׂר כִּי לְעוֹלָם חַסְדּוֹ. וּבְטוּבוֹ הַגָּדוֹל תָּמִיד לֹא חָסַר לָנוּ וְאַל יֶחְסַר לָנוּ מָזוֹן לְעוֹלָם וָעֶד בַּעֲבוּר שְׁמוֹ הַגָּדוֹל, כִּי הוּא זָן וּמְפַרְנֵס לַכֹּל וּמֵטִיב לַכֹּל וּמֵכִין מָזוֹן לְכָל־בְּרִיּוֹתָיו אֲשֶׁר בָּרָא. בָּרוּךְ אַתָּה יְיָ, הַזָּן אֶת־הַכֹּל.

נוֹדֶה לְּךָ יְיָ אֱלֹהֵינוּ עַל שֶׁהִנְחַלְתָּ לַאֲבוֹתֵינוּ אֶרֶץ חֶמְדָּה טוֹבָה וּרְחָבָה, וְעַל שֶׁהוֹצֵאתָנוּ יְיָ אֱלֹהֵינוּ מֵאֶרֶץ מִצְרַיִם, וּפְדִיתָנוּ מִבֵּית עֲבָדִים, וְעַל בְּרִיתְךָ שֶׁחָתַמְתָּ בִּבְשָׂרֵנוּ, וְעַל תּוֹרָתְךָ שֶׁלִּמַּדְתָּנוּ, וְעַל חֻקֶּיךָ שֶׁהוֹדַעְתָּנוּ, וְעַל חַיִּים חֵן וָחֶסֶד שֶׁחוֹנַנְתָּנוּ, וְעַל אֲכִילַת מָזוֹן שָׁאַתָּה זָן וּמְפַרְנֵס אוֹתָנוּ תָּמִיד, בְּכָל־יוֹם וּבְכָל־עֵת וּבְכָל־שָׁעָה.

וְעַל הַכֹּל יְיָ אֱלֹהֵינוּ אֲנַחְנוּ מוֹדִים לָךְ וּמְבָרְכִים אוֹתָךְ. יִתְבָּרַךְ שִׁמְךָ בְּפִי כָל־חַי תָּמִיד לְעוֹלָם וָעֶד, כַּכָּתוּב: וְאָכַלְתָּ וְשָׂבָעְתָּ וּבֵרַכְתָּ אֶת־יְיָ אֱלֹהֶיךָ עַל הָאָרֶץ הַטּוֹבָה אֲשֶׁר נָתַן לָךְ. בָּרוּךְ אַתָּה יְיָ, עַל הָאָרֶץ וְעַל הַמָּזוֹן.

רַחֵם יְיָ אֱלֹהֵינוּ עַל יִשְׂרָאֵל עַמֶּךָ, וְעַל יְרוּשָׁלַיִם עִירֶךָ, וְעַל צִיּוֹן מִשְׁכַּן כְּבוֹדֶךָ, וְעַל מַלְכוּת בֵּית דָּוִד מְשִׁיחֶךָ, וְעַל הַבַּיִת הַגָּדוֹל וְהַקָּדוֹשׁ שֶׁנִּקְרָא שִׁמְךָ עָלָיו. אֱלֹהֵינוּ אָבִינוּ, רְעֵנוּ זוּנֵנוּ, פַּרְנְסֵנוּ וְכַלְכְּלֵנוּ וְהַרְוִיחֵנוּ, וְהַרְוַח לָנוּ יְיָ אֱלֹהֵינוּ מְהֵרָה מִכָּל־צָרוֹתֵינוּ. וְנָא אַל תַּצְרִיכֵנוּ יְיָ אֱלֹהֵינוּ לֹא לִידֵי מַתְּנַת בָּשָׂר וָדָם וְלֹא לִידֵי הַלְוָאָתָם, כִּי אִם לְיָדְךָ הַמְּלֵאָה הַפְּתוּחָה הַגְּדוּשָׁה וְהָרְחָבָה, שֶׁלֹּא נֵבוֹשׁ וְלֹא נִכָּלֵם לְעוֹלָם וָעֶד.

רְצֵה וְהַחֲלִיצֵנוּ יְיָ אֱלֹהֵינוּ בְּמִצְוֹתֶיךָ, וּבְמִצְוַת יוֹם הַשְּׁבִיעִי הַשַּׁבָּת הַגָּדוֹל וְהַקָּדוֹשׁ הַזֶּה כִּי יוֹם זֶה גָּדוֹל וְקָדוֹשׁ הוּא לְפָנֶיךָ לִשְׁבָּת־בּוֹ וְלָנוּחַ בּוֹ בְּאַהֲבָה כְּמִצְוַת רְצוֹנֶךָ. בִּרְצוֹנְךָ הָנַח לָנוּ יְיָ אֱלֹהֵינוּ שֶׁלֹּא תְהִי צָרָה וְיָגוֹן וַאֲנָחָה בְּיוֹם מְנוּחָתֵנוּ, וְהַרְאֵנוּ יְיָ אֱלֹהֵינוּ בְּנֶחָמַת צִיּוֹן עִירֶךָ, וּבְבִנְיַן יְרוּשָׁלַיִם עִיר קָדְשֶׁךָ, כִּי אַתָּה הוּא בַּעַל הַיְשׁוּעוֹת וּבַעַל הַנֶּחָמוֹת.

וּבְנֵה יְרוּשָׁלַיִם עִיר הַקֹּדֶשׁ בִּמְהֵרָה בְיָמֵינוּ. בָּרוּךְ אַתָּה יְיָ, בּוֹנֵה בְרַחֲמָיו יְרוּשָׁלַיִם. אָמֵן.

Praised are You, Lord our God, King of the universe who sustains the whole world with kindness and with compassion. He provides food for every creature, for His love endures forever. His great goodness has never failed us, His great glory assures us nourishment. All life is His creation and He is good to all, providing every creature with food and sustenance. Praised are You, Lord who sustains all life.

We thank You, Lord our God, for the pleasing, ample, desirable land which You gave to our ancestors, and for liberating us from Egyptian bondage. We thank You for the covenant sealed in our flesh, for teaching us Your Torah and its precepts, for the gift of life so graciously granted us, for the food we have eaten, for the nourishment You provide us all our days, whatever the season, whatever the time.

For all this we thank You and praise You, Lord our God. May You forever be praised by all who live, as it is written in the Torah: "When you have eaten and are satisfied, you shall praise the Lord your God for the good land which He has given you." Praised are You, Lord, for the land and for sustenance.

Lord our God, have mercy for Your people Israel, Jerusalem Your city, Zion the home of Your glory, the kingdom of the House of David Your anointed, and the great and holy House which is called by Your name. Our God, our Father, sustain us, maintain us, grant us encouragement as well as our nourishment; grant us relief from all our troubles. May we never find ourselves in need of gifts or loans from flesh and blood, but may we always rely only upon Your helping hand, which is open and generous; thus we will never be humiliated or put to shame.

Please give us the strength, Lord our God, to observe Your commandments, especially the commandment of this great and holy seventh day, that we may rest thereon, willingly, as You have graciously commanded. May it be Your will, Lord our God, to grant that our Shabbat rest be free of sorrow, anguish, and distress. May we behold Zion Your city consoled, Lord our God, and Jerusalem Your holy city rebuilt. For You are the Lord of deliverance and consolation.

Fully rebuild Jerusalem, the holy city, soon, in our time. Praised are You, Lord who in His mercy rebuilds Jerusalem. Amen.

בָּרוּךְ אַתָּה יְיָ אֱלֹהֵינוּ מֶלֶךְ הָעוֹלָם, הָאֵל אָבִינוּ מַלְכֵּנוּ אַדִּירֵנוּ
בּוֹרְאֵנוּ גּוֹאֲלֵנוּ יוֹצְרֵנוּ קְדוֹשֵׁנוּ קְדוֹשׁ יַעֲקֹב, רוֹעֵנוּ רוֹעֵה יִשְׂרָאֵל,
הַמֶּלֶךְ הַטּוֹב וְהַמֵּטִיב לַכֹּל, שֶׁבְּכָל־יוֹם וָיוֹם הוּא הֵטִיב, הוּא
מֵטִיב, הוּא יֵיטִיב לָנוּ. הוּא גְמָלָנוּ הוּא גוֹמְלֵנוּ הוּא יִגְמְלֵנוּ לָעַד,
לְחֵן לְחֶסֶד וּלְרַחֲמִים וּלְרֶוַח הַצָּלָה וְהַצְלָחָה, בְּרָכָה וִישׁוּעָה
נֶחָמָה פַּרְנָסָה וְכַלְכָּלָה וְרַחֲמִים וְחַיִּים וְשָׁלוֹם וְכָל־טוֹב, וּמִכָּל־
טוּב אַל יְחַסְּרֵנוּ.

הָרַחֲמָן, הוּא יִמְלֹךְ עָלֵינוּ לְעוֹלָם וָעֶד.

הָרַחֲמָן, הוּא יִתְבָּרַךְ בַּשָּׁמַיִם וּבָאָרֶץ.

הָרַחֲמָן, הוּא יִשְׁתַּבַּח לְדוֹר דּוֹרִים, וְיִתְפָּאַר בָּנוּ לָעַד וּלְנֵצַח
נְצָחִים, וְיִתְהַדַּר בָּנוּ לָעַד וּלְעוֹלְמֵי עוֹלָמִים.

הָרַחֲמָן, הוּא יְפַרְנְסֵנוּ בְּכָבוֹד.

הָרַחֲמָן, הוּא יִשְׁבֹּר עֻלֵּנוּ מֵעַל צַוָּארֵנוּ, וְהוּא יוֹלִיכֵנוּ קוֹמְמִיּוּת
לְאַרְצֵנוּ.

הָרַחֲמָן, הוּא יִשְׁלַח בְּרָכָה מְרֻבָּה בַּבַּיִת הַזֶּה, וְעַל שֻׁלְחָן זֶה
שֶׁאָכַלְנוּ עָלָיו.

הָרַחֲמָן, הוּא יְבָרֵךְ אֶת־הָאָרֶץ הַזֹּאת וְיָגֵן עָלֶיהָ.

הָרַחֲמָן, הוּא יְבָרֵךְ אֶת־מְדִינַת יִשְׂרָאֵל, רֵאשִׁית צְמִיחַת גְּאֻלָּתֵנוּ.

הָרַחֲמָן, הוּא יְבָרֵךְ אֶת־אַחֵינוּ בְּנֵי יִשְׂרָאֵל הַנְּתוּנִים בְּצָרָה
וְיוֹצִיאֵם מֵאֲפֵלָה לְאוֹרָה.

Praised are You, Lord our God, King of the universe, our Father, our King, our Creator and Redeemer who fashioned us, our Holy One and the Holy One of Jacob, our Shepherd and Shepherd of the people Israel, the King who is good to all, whose goodness is constant throughout all time. Bestow upon us grace, kindness, and compassion, providing us deliverance, prosperity and ease, life and peace and all goodness. May we never lack any goodness.

May the Merciful reign over us throughout all time.

May the Merciful be praised in heaven and on earth.

May the Merciful be lauded in every generation, glorified through our lives, exalted through us always and to all eternity.

May the Merciful give us an honorable livelihood.

May the Merciful break the yoke about our necks and lead us in dignity to our land.

May the Merciful send a full measure of blessing to this house and to this table at which we have eaten.

May the Merciful bless this land and protect it.

May the Merciful bless the State of Israel, the dawn of our redemption.

May the Merciful bless all our people who suffer, and bring them out of darkness into light.

At home:

הָרַחֲמָן, הוּא יְבָרֵךְ אֶת־(אָבִי) בַּעַל הַבַּיִת הַזֶּה וְאֶת־(אִמִּי) בַּעֲלַת הַבַּיִת הַזֶּה, אוֹתָם וְאֶת־בֵּיתָם וְאֶת־זַרְעָם וְאֶת־כָּל־אֲשֶׁר לָהֶם.

At public gatherings:

הָרַחֲמָן, הוּא יְבָרֵךְ אֶת־כָּל־הַמְסֻבִּים כָּאן.

אוֹתָנוּ וְאֶת־כָּל־אֲשֶׁר לָנוּ, כְּמוֹ שֶׁנִּתְבָּרְכוּ אֲבוֹתֵינוּ אַבְרָהָם יִצְחָק וְיַעֲקֹב בַּכֹּל מִכֹּל כֹּל. כֵּן יְבָרֵךְ אוֹתָנוּ כֻּלָּנוּ יַחַד בִּבְרָכָה שְׁלֵמָה, וְנֹאמַר אָמֵן.

בַּמָּרוֹם יְלַמְּדוּ עֲלֵיהֶם וְעָלֵינוּ זְכוּת שֶׁתְּהִי לְמִשְׁמֶרֶת שָׁלוֹם. וְנִשָּׂא בְרָכָה מֵאֵת יְיָ וּצְדָקָה מֵאֱלֹהֵי יִשְׁעֵנוּ, וְנִמְצָא חֵן וְשֵׂכֶל טוֹב בְּעֵינֵי אֱלֹהִים וְאָדָם.

הָרַחֲמָן, הוּא יַנְחִילֵנוּ יוֹם שֶׁכֻּלּוֹ שַׁבָּת וּמְנוּחָה לְחַיֵּי הָעוֹלָמִים.

הָרַחֲמָן הוּא יְזַכֵּנוּ לִימוֹת הַמָּשִׁיחַ וּלְחַיֵּי הָעוֹלָם הַבָּא. מִגְדּוֹל יְשׁוּעוֹת מַלְכּוֹ וְעֹשֶׂה חֶסֶד לִמְשִׁיחוֹ לְדָוִד וּלְזַרְעוֹ עַד עוֹלָם. עֹשֶׂה שָׁלוֹם בִּמְרוֹמָיו הוּא יַעֲשֶׂה שָׁלוֹם עָלֵינוּ וְעַל כָּל־יִשְׂרָאֵל וְאִמְרוּ אָמֵן.

יְראוּ אֶת־יהוה קְדֹשָׁיו, כִּי אֵין מַחְסוֹר לִירֵאָיו. כְּפִירִים רָשׁוּ וְרָעֵבוּ, וְדֹרְשֵׁי יהוה לֹא יַחְסְרוּ כָל־טוֹב. הוֹדוּ לַיהוה כִּי טוֹב, כִּי לְעוֹלָם חַסְדּוֹ. פּוֹתֵחַ אֶת־יָדֶךָ וּמַשְׂבִּיעַ לְכָל־חַי רָצוֹן. בָּרוּךְ הַגֶּבֶר אֲשֶׁר יִבְטַח בַּיהוה, וְהָיָה יהוה מִבְטַחוֹ. נַעַר הָיִיתִי גַּם זָקַנְתִּי וְלֹא רָאִיתִי צַדִּיק נֶעֱזָב וְזַרְעוֹ מְבַקֶּשׁ־לָחֶם. יהוה עֹז לְעַמּוֹ יִתֵּן, יהוה יְבָרֵךְ אֶת־עַמּוֹ בַשָּׁלוֹם.

At home:

May the Merciful bless (my father) the master of this house, and (my mother) the mistress of this house, together with their children and all that is theirs.

At public gatherings:

May the Merciful bless all who are gathered here.

May He bless us and all that is ours, as He blessed our fathers, Abraham, Isaac, and Jacob, in everything. May He bless us all together, fully. And let us say: Amen.

May grace and merit be invoked on high for them and for us, leading to enduring peace. May we receive blessings from the Lord, lovingkindness from the God of our deliverance. May we find grace and good favor before God and all people.

May the Merciful grant us a day of true Shabbat rest, reflecting the life of eternity.

May the Merciful consider us worthy of the messianic era, and life in the world to come. He gives great salvation to His king, lovingkindness to His anointed, to David and to his descendants forevermore. May He who brings peace to His universe bring peace to us, and to all the people Israel. And let us say: Amen.

Revere the Lord, you His holy ones; for those who revere Him know no want. Even young lions lack, and suffer hunger, but those who seek Adonai shall not lack any good thing. Give thanks to the Lord, for He is good; His love endures forever. He opens His hand and satisfies every living thing with favor. Blessed is the man who trusts in the Lord, whose trust the Lord is. I have been young and now I am old; yet I have not seen the righteous forsaken, nor his children begging for bread. May the Lord grant His people dignity; may the Lord bless His people with peace.

Short Version

בִּרְכַּת הַמָּזוֹן

Birkat Hamazon
Blessings After the Meal

שִׁיר הַמַּעֲלוֹת בְּשׁוּב יהוה אֶת־שִׁיבַת צִיּוֹן הָיִינוּ כְּחֹלְמִים. אָז יִמָּלֵא שְׂחוֹק פִּינוּ וּלְשׁוֹנֵנוּ רִנָּה. אָז יֹאמְרוּ בַגּוֹיִם הִגְדִּיל יהוה לַעֲשׂוֹת עִם אֵלֶּה. הִגְדִּיל יהוה לַעֲשׂוֹת עִמָּנוּ הָיִינוּ שְׂמֵחִים. שׁוּבָה יהוה אֶת־שְׁבִיתֵנוּ כַּאֲפִיקִים בַּנֶּגֶב. הַזֹּרְעִים בְּדִמְעָה בְּרִנָּה יִקְצֹרוּ. הָלוֹךְ יֵלֵךְ וּבָכֹה נֹשֵׂא מֶשֶׁךְ הַזָּרַע בֹּא יָבֹא בְרִנָּה נֹשֵׂא אֲלֻמֹּתָיו.

Shir hama'alot beshuv Adonai et shivat tziyon, hayinu kecholmim. Az yimalei sechok pinu, uleshoneinu rinah. Az yomru vagoyim, higdil Adonai la'asot im ayleh. Higdil Adonai la'asot imanu, ha'yinu semeichim. Shuvah Adonai et sheviteinu, ka'afikim banegev. Hazore'im bedimah berinah yik-tzoru. Halokh yeileikh uvakho nosei meshekh hazara. Bo yavo verinah nosei alumotav.

When the Lord brought our exiles back to Zion, it was like a dream. Then our mouths were filled with laughter, joyous song was on our tongues. Then it was said among the nations: "The Lord has done great things for them." Great things indeed He did for us; therefore we rejoiced. Bring us back, O Lord, as You bring streams back to Israel's desert soil. Those who sow in tears shall reap with joyous song. A hungry man will plant in sadness, bearing his few sacks of seed; but he will come back home in gladness, bearing ample sheaves of grain.

When three or more adults have eaten together, one of them formally invites the others to join in these blessings. (When ten or more are present, add the words in parentheses.)

רַבּוֹתַי נְבָרֵךְ.

Rabotai nevarekh.
Friends, let us give thanks.

The others respond, and the leader repeats:

יְהִי שֵׁם יְיָ מְבֹרָךְ מֵעַתָּה וְעַד עוֹלָם.

Yehi shem Adonai mevorakh mei-attah v'ad olam.
May the Lord be praised, now and forever.

The leader continues:

בִּרְשׁוּת רַבּוֹתַי, נְבָרֵךְ (אֱלֹהֵינוּ) שֶׁאָכַלְנוּ מִשֶּׁלּוֹ.

Bir'shut rabotai, n'varekh (elo-heinu) sheh-akhalnu mi-shelo.
With your consent, friends, let us praise (our God) the One of whose food
we have partaken.

The others respond, and the leader repeats:

בָּרוּךְ (אֱלֹהֵינוּ) שֶׁאָכַלְנוּ מִשֶּׁלּוֹ וּבְטוּבוֹ חָיִינוּ.

Barukh (elo-heinu) sheh-akhalnu mi-shelo uve-tuvo chayinu.
Praised be (our God) the One of whose food we have partaken and by
whose goodness we live.

Leader and others:

בָּרוּךְ הוּא וּבָרוּךְ שְׁמוֹ.

Barukh hu u-varukh sh'mo.
Praised be He and praised be His name.

בָּרוּךְ אַתָּה יְיָ אֱלֹהֵינוּ מֶלֶךְ הָעוֹלָם, הַזָּן אֶת־הָעוֹלָם כֻּלּוֹ בְּטוּבוֹ,
בְּחֵן בְּחֶסֶד וּבְרַחֲמִים. הוּא נוֹתֵן לֶחֶם לְכָל־בָּשָׂר כִּי לְעוֹלָם חַסְדּוֹ.
וּבְטוּבוֹ הַגָּדוֹל תָּמִיד לֹא חָסַר לָנוּ וְאַל יֶחְסַר לָנוּ מָזוֹן לְעוֹלָם וָעֶד
בַּעֲבוּר שְׁמוֹ הַגָּדוֹל, כִּי הוּא זָן וּמְפַרְנֵס לַכֹּל וּמֵטִיב לַכֹּל וּמֵכִין
מָזוֹן לְכָל־בְּרִיּוֹתָיו אֲשֶׁר בָּרָא. בָּרוּךְ אַתָּה יְיָ, הַזָּן אֶת־הַכֹּל.

Barukh atah Adonai, Elohaynu melekh ha'olam, hazan et ha'olam kulo betuvo, bechein, bechesed, uverachamim. Hu notayn lechem lekhol basar, ki le'olam chasdo. Uvetuvo hagadol, tamid lo chasar lanu, ve'al yechsar lanu mazon le'olam va'ed ba'avur shemo hagadol, ki hu zan umefarneis lakol, umaytiv lakol, umaykhim mazon lekhol beriyotav asher bara. Barukh atah Adonai, hazan et hakol.

Praised are You, Lord our God, King of the universe who sustains the whole world with kindness and compassion. He provides food for every creature, for His love endures forever. His great goodness has never failed us. His great glory assures us nourishment. All life is His creation and He is good to all, providing every creature with food and sustenance. Praised are You, Lord who sustains all life.

נוֹדֶה לְךָ יְיָ אֱלֹהֵינוּ עַל שֶׁהִנְחַלְתָּ לַאֲבוֹתֵינוּ אֶרֶץ חֶמְדָּה טוֹבָה וּרְחָבָה, בְּרִית וְתוֹרָה, חַיִּים וּמָזוֹן. יִתְבָּרַךְ שִׁמְךָ בְּפִי כָל־חַי תָּמִיד לְעוֹלָם וָעֶד, כַּכָּתוּב: וְאָכַלְתָּ וְשָׂבָעְתָּ וּבֵרַכְתָּ אֶת־יְיָ אֱלֹהֶיךָ עַל הָאָרֶץ הַטּוֹבָה אֲשֶׁר נָתַן לָךְ. בָּרוּךְ אַתָּה יְיָ, עַל הָאָרֶץ וְעַל הַמָּזוֹן.

Nodeh lekha Adonai Eloheinu al shehinchalta la'avoteinu eretz chemdah, tovah urechavah, brit vetorah, cha'yim umazon. Yitbarakh shimkha befi khol chai tamid le'olam va'ed. Kakatuv ve'akhalta vesavata uveirakhta et Adonai Elohekha al ha'aretz hatovah asher natan lakh. Barukh atah Adonai, al ha'aretz ve'al hamazon.

We thank You, Lord our God, for the pleasing, ample, desirable land which You gave to our ancestors, for the covenant and Torah, for life and sustenance. May You forever be praised by all who who live, as it is written in the Torah: "When you have eaten and are satisfied, you shall praise the Lord your God for the good land which He has given you." Praised are You, Lord, for the land and for sustenance.

וּבְנֵה יְרוּשָׁלַיִם עִיר הַקֹּדֶשׁ בִּמְהֵרָה בְיָמֵינוּ. בָּרוּךְ אַתָּה יְיָ, בֹּנֵה בְרַחֲמָיו יְרוּשָׁלָיִם. אָמֵן.

בָּרוּךְ אַתָּה יְיָ אֱלֹהֵינוּ מֶלֶךְ הָעוֹלָם, הַמֶּלֶךְ הַטּוֹב וְהַמֵּטִיב לַכֹּל. הוּא הֵטִיב, הוּא מֵטִיב, הוּא יֵיטִיב לָנוּ. הוּא גְמָלָנוּ הוּא גוֹמְלֵנוּ הוּא יִגְמְלֵנוּ לָעַד חֵן חֶסֶד וְרַחֲמִים וִיזַכֵּנוּ לִימוֹת הַמָּשִׁיחַ.

Uvenei Yerushalayim ir hakodesh bimhayrah ve'yameinu. Barukh atah Adonai, boneh verachamav Yerushala'yim. Amen.

Barukh atah Adonai, Eloheinu melekh ha'olam, hamelekh hatov vehamei-tiv lakol. Hu heitiv, hu meitiv, hu yeitiv lanu. Hu gemalanu, hu gomlaynu, hu yigmileinu la'ad hein vachesed verachamim, viyzakeinu liymot ha-mashiach.

Fully rebuild Jerusalem, the holy city, soon, in our time. Praised are You, Lord who in His mercy rebuilds Jerusalem. Amen.

Praised are You, Lord our God, King of the universe who is good to all, whose goodness is constant throughout all time. Favor us with kindness and compassion now and in the future as in the past. May, we be worthy of the days of the messiah.

הָרַחֲמָן, הוּא יַנְחִילֵנוּ יוֹם שֶׁכֻּלוֹ שַׁבָּת וּמְנוּחָה לְחַיֵּי הָעוֹלָמִים.

וְנִשָּׂא בְרָכָה מֵאֵת יְיָ וּצְדָקָה מֵאֱלֹהֵי יִשְׁעֵנוּ וְנִמְצָא חֵן וְשֵׂכֶל טוֹב בְּעֵינֵי אֱלֹהִים וְאָדָם. עֹשֶׂה שָׁלוֹם בִּמְרוֹמָיו הוּא יַעֲשֶׂה שָׁלוֹם עָלֵינוּ וְעַל כָּל־יִשְׂרָאֵל, וְאִמְרוּ אָמֵן.

Harachaman hu yanchileinu yom shekuylo Shabbat umenuchah lechayei ha'olamim.

Venisa verakhah mei'eit Adonai, utzedakah mei'Elohei yisheinu. Venimtza chein veseichel tov be'einei Elohim ve'adam. Oseh shalom bimromav hu y'aseh shalom aleinu ve'al kol Yisrael. Ve'imru Amen.

May the Merciful grant us a day of true Shabbat rest, reflecting the life of eternity.

May we receive blessings from the Lord, lovingkindness from the God of our deliverance. May we find grace and good favor before God and all people. May He who brings peace to His universe bring peace to us and to all the people Israel. And let us say: Amen.

Talmud Torah—Study

The importance of the study of Torah is emphasized over and over again in Jewish tradition. To cite just two examples:

> Three who have eaten together at one table and spoken words of Torah, it is as if they had eaten at the table of God (Ethics of the Fathers 3:4).

> These are the things for which no limit is prescribed: the corner of the field, the first-fruits, the pilgrimage offerings, the practice of kindness, and the study of the Torah. These are the things of which a man enjoys the fruits in this world, while the principal remains for him in the hereafter, namely: honoring father and mother, practice of kindness, early attendance at the schoolhouse morning and evening, hospitality to strangers, visiting the sick, dowering the bride, attending the dead to the grave, devotion in prayer, and making peace between fellow men; but the study of the Torah excels them all (Peah 1:1; Talmud Shabbath 127a).

We begin our study tonight by reciting the following blessing:

בָּרוּךְ אַתָּה יְיָ אֱלֹהֵינוּ מֶלֶךְ הָעוֹלָם,
אֲשֶׁר קִדְּשָׁנוּ בְּמִצְוֹתָיו וְצִוָּנוּ לַעֲסֹק בְּדִבְרֵי תוֹרָה.

Praised are You, Lord our God, King of the universe, who has sanctified our lives through His commandments, commanding us to study Torah.

Concluding Prayer

וְהַעֲרֶב־נָא יְיָ אֱלֹהֵינוּ אֶת דִּבְרֵי תוֹרָתְךָ בְּפִינוּ, וּבְפִי עַמְּךָ בֵּית
יִשְׂרָאֵל, וְנִהְיֶה אֲנַחְנוּ וְצֶאֱצָאֵינוּ, וְצֶאֱצָאֵי עַמְּךָ בֵּית יִשְׂרָאֵל, כֻּלָּנוּ
יוֹדְעֵי שְׁמֶךָ וְלוֹמְדֵי תוֹרָתֶךָ לִשְׁמָהּ. בָּרוּךְ אַתָּה יְיָ, הַמְלַמֵּד תּוֹרָה
לְעַמּוֹ יִשְׂרָאֵל:

Lord our God, make the words of Your Torah pleasant in our mouths and in the mouths of Your people Israel, so that we and our descendants and all the descendants of Your people Israel may know Your name and study Torah for its own sake. Praised are You, Lord, who teaches Torah to His people Israel.

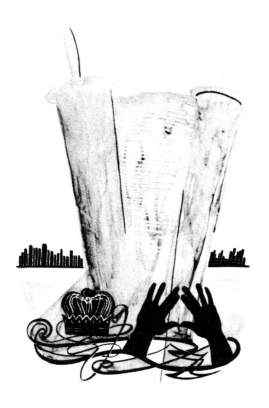

PART II

Shabbat Study Texts

UNIT I

the meaning of shabbat

The concept of Shabbat and its unique value for Jews is illustrated in the story *The Treasure* by Isaac Leib Peretz. Peretz (1852–1915) was one of the founders of modern Yiddish literature, together with Mendele Mokher Sforim and Sholem Aleichem. His stories portray the lives of Hasidim and of the common people of Eastern Europe.

The Treasure[7]

By Isaac Leib Peretz

To sleep in summer time in a room four yards square, together with a wife and eight children, is anything but a pleasure. Even on a Friday night. So Shmerel, the woodcutter, rises hot and gasping from his bed, and, though only half through with the night, hastily pours some water over his finger-tips, flings on his dressing gown and escapes barefoot from the parched *Gehenna* of his dwelling. He steps into the street. All is quiet, all the shutters are closed, and over the sleeping town stretches a distant, serene, and starry sky. He feels as if he were all alone with God, blessed be He, and he says, looking up at the sky, "Now, Lord of the Universe, now is the time to hear me and to bless me with a treasure out of Thy treasure-house!"

As he says this, he sees something like a little flame coming along out of the town, and he knows that that is the treasure! He is about to pursue it when he remembers that it is Sabbath when one must not run. So he goes after it walking. And as he walks slowly along, the little flame begins to move slowly, too, so that the distance between them does not increase, though it does not decrease, either. He walks on. Now and then an inward voice calls to him: "Shmerel, don't be a fool! Take off the dressing gown, jump and throw it over the flame!" But he knows it is the Evil Inclination speaking. He throws the dressing gown onto his arm, but to spite the Evil

43

Inclination he takes still smaller steps and rejoices to see that, as soon as he takes these smaller steps, the little flame moves more slowly, too.

Thus he follows and follows the flame till he gradually finds himself outside the town. The road twists and turns across fields and meadows, and the distance between him and the flame grows no longer, no shorter. Were he to throw the dressing gown now it would not reach the flame. Meantime the thought revolves in his mind: Were he indeed to become possessed of the treasure, he would no longer have to be a woodcutter in his old age; truly he no longer has the strength for such work. Then he would rent a seat for his wife in the women's *Shool*, so that her Sabbaths and holidays should not be spoiled by not being allowed to sit here or sit there. On New Year's Day and the Day of Atonement it is all she can do to stand through the service. Her many children have exhausted her! And he would have a new dress made for her and buy her a few strings of pearls. The children should be sent to better *Hadarim*, and he would cast about for a match for his eldest girl. As it is, the poor child carries her mother's fruit baskets and never has time so much as to comb her hair thoroughly. And she has long, long plaits, and eyes like a deer.

"It would be a meritorious act to pounce upon the treasure!"

The Evil Inclination speaks again, he thinks. If it is not to be, well, then it is not to be! If it were a weekday, he would soon know what to do! Or if his Yainkel were here he would have something to say. Children nowadays! Who knows what they don't do on the Sabbath! And the younger one is no better. He makes fun of the teacher in *Heder*. When the teacher is about to administer a blow they pull his beard. And who's going to find time to look after them—chopping and sawing the whole day through.

He sighs and walks on and on, now and then glancing up into the sky. "Lord of the Universe, of whom are you making trial? Shmerel Woodcutter? If you mean to give me the treasure, *give* it to me!" It seems to him that the flame advances more slowly. But at this moment he hears a dog barking and recognizes the bark as that of the dog in Vissoke. Vissoke is the first village you come to on leaving the town. He sees white patches twinkling in the dewy morning atmosphere. Those are the Vissoke peasant cottages. Then it occurs to him that he has gone a Sabbath day's journey and he stops short.

"Yes, I have gone a Sabbath day's journey," he thinks, and says, speaking into the air: "You won't lead me astray! It is *not* a Godsend! God does not make sport of us. It is the work of a demon." And he feels a little angry with the thing and turns and hurries toward the town, thinking: "I won't say anything about it at home, because, first, they won't believe me, and if they do, they'll laugh at me. And what have I done to be proud of? The Creator knows how it was, and that is enough for me. Besides, *she* might be angry, who can tell? The children are certainly naked and barefoot, poor little things! Why should they be made to transgress the commandment to honor one's father?"

No, he won't breathe a word of it. He won't even remind the Almighty of it. If he really has been good, the Almighty will remember without being told.

And suddenly he is conscious of a strange, inward calm, and there is a delicious sensation in his limbs. Money is, after all, dross. Riches may even lead a man from the right way. And he feels inclined to thank God for not having brought him into temptation by granting him his wish. Now he would like to sing a song! "Our Father, our King" is one he remembers from his early years, but he feels ashamed and breaks off. He tries to recollect one of the cantor's melodies, a Sinai tune, when suddenly he sees that the little flame which he left behind him is once more preceding him, and moving slowly townward, townward. And the distance between them neither increases nor diminishes, as though the flame were taking a walk, and he were taking a walk, just taking a little walk in honor of the Sabbath. He is glad in his heart and watches it. The sky pales, the stars begin to fade, the east flushes, a narrow pink stream flows lengthwise over his head, and still the flame flickers onward into the town, enters his own street. There is his house. The door, he sees, is open. Apparently he forgot to shut it. And, lo and behold! the flame goes in, the flame goes through his own house door! He follows and sees it disappear under the bed. All are asleep. He goes softly up to the bed, stoops down, and sees the flame spinning round underneath, like a top, always in the same place. He takes his dressing gown, throws it under the bed, and covers the flame. No one hears him. And now a golden morning beam steals in through the chink in the shutter.

He sits down on the bed and makes a vow not to say a word to anyone till Sabbath is over—not half a word, lest it cause desecration of the Sabbath. *She* could never hold her tongue, and the children certainly could not. They would at once want to count the treasure, to know how much there was, and very soon the secret would be out of the house and in the *Shool*, the house-of-study, and all about the streets. And people would talk about his treasure, about his luck. They would not say their prayers, or wash their hands, or say grace, as they should. And he would have led his household and half the town into sin. No, not a whisper! And he stretches himself out on the bed and pretends to be asleep.

And this was his reward: When, after concluding the Sabbath, he stooped down and lifted the dressing gown there lay a sack with a million gulden in it!

And he lived happily all the years of his life.

Only his wife was continually throwing it up to him: "Lord of the World, how could a man have such a heart of stone as to sit a whole summer day and not say a word, not a word, not to his own wife, not one single word! And there was I crying over my prayer as I said God of Abraham— and crying so—for there wasn't a penny left in the house."

Then he would console her, and say with a smile:

"Who knows? Perhaps it was all thanks to your prayer—'God of Abraham'—that it went off so well."

Explanatory Note

"A Sabbath day's journey." There is a prohibition on Shabbat against traveling more than a certain distance (two thousand *amot*) outside a town. If Shmerel had gone any farther, it would have been a transgression.

Questions for Discussion

What does this story tell us about Shmerel's relationship to God? To Shabbat?

What does it tell us about the life of the Jewish community in Eastern Europe?

What is the "treasure" to which the title of the story refers?

Do you think the "treasure" of the title might refer to something other than money?

Why do you think Shmerel got the treasure? What was it a reward for?

Should he have told his wife about the treasure?

Do you think he received the treasure because of his wife's prayers?

What is the meaning of the last line?

Suggested Questions for Children

Would you have taken the treasure right away? If you were poor, would that make a difference?

If you knew there was a treasure under your bed, do you think you could keep it a secret for a whole day?

Do you think Shmerel should have kept it a secret? Was he wrong not to trust his family?

We close our Shabbat study with the concluding prayer on page 40.

UNIT II

the Relationship
Between God and people

This unit is built around the Tower of Babel story from Genesis (11:1–9). There is also a supplementary reading, a *midrash* which retells the biblical story.

> All the earth had the same language and the same words. And as men migrated from the east, they came upon a valley in the land of Shinar and settled there. They said to one another, "Come, let us make bricks and burn them hard." Brick served them as stone, and bitumen served them as mortar. And they said, "Come let us build us a city, and a tower with its top in the sky, to make a name for ourselves; else we shall be scattered all over the world."
>
> The Lord came down to look at the city and tower which man had built, and the Lord said, "If, as one people with one language for all, this is how they have begun to act, then nothing that they may propose to do will be out of their reach. Let us, then, go down and confound their speech there, so they shall not understand one another's speech."
>
> Thus the Lord scattered them from there over the face of the whole earth; and they stopped building the city. That is why it was called Babel, because there the Lord confounded the speech of the whole earth; and from there the Lord scattered them over the face of the whole earth.

Explanatory Notes

"Let us, then, go down." The Midrash (traditional Jewish exegesis) interprets this as God talking to the angels. Biblical scholars say the use of the plural reflects pre-Israelite belief in a multiplicity of gods. This use of the plural is also found in Genesis 1:26, "Let us make man in our image."

"Babel . . . the Lord confounded." The Hebrew word *balal*, "confounded," is a play upon the word Babel.

47

The Generation of the Divison of Tongues[8]

From the Midrash

Now in the whole world they had one language and the same words. And all the princes of Nimrod and his great men took counsel at that time, these being Put and Mitzrayim and Kush and Canaan after their families. And they said to one another: "Come, let us build ourselves a city, with a strong and buttressed tower within it whose top reaches the very skies. In that way we shall give ourselves a name in order that we may become the rulers over the whole world and the evil of our foes may depart from us; and we shall be able to rule over them by force and not be scattered all over the earth because of their wars."

So they all went and came before the king and told him this counsel, and the king thanked them for it. And they did this. All the families gathered together, about six hundred thousand men in all, and they went to seek for a very broad and spacious land in which to build the city and the tower. They searched all over the earth and found no place so suitable as a certain valley lying toward the east in the land of Shinar, a two years' journey. And they all traveled thither and dwelt there.

They then began to fashion bricks and to bake them in order to build the city and the tower they planned. And the building of the tower became a sin and transgression to them, as they began to build it. For while they were building it, they rebelled against the Lord God of Heaven, thinking in their hearts to wage war against Him and go up into the heavens, and all these men and families split into three groups. One said: "Let us go up to heaven and wage war against Him." The next said: "Let us go up to heaven and place our gods there and do service to them on high." And the third group said: "Let us go up to heaven and smite Him with bows and lances."

Now God knew all their deeds and evil thoughts and saw the city and tower that they were building. In the course of the construction they built themselves a large city and within it an exceedingly lofty and powerful tower. For by reason of the height, the mortar and the bricks could not reach the builder when they climbed up to him until they had spent a full year at the climbing. Only after that could they reach the builders and give them the mortar and the bricks.

This they would do for them day after day, so that some were always climbing up and others were climbing down all day long. Furthermore, if a brick fell from their hands and broke, they all wept. But if a man fell and perished, not one of them would look at him or be concerned.

48

Now the Lord knew their thoughts. While they were building, they shot arrows at the sky and all the arrows fell back drenched in blood. When they saw this, they said to one another: "Why, we have slain all who are in the heavens." For this was done by the Lord in order to mislead them and destroy them from off the face of the earth.

And the Lord said to the seventy angels who stand first before Him and are closest to Him: "Come, let us go down and confuse their speech below, so that no man should be able to understand the speech of his friend." And this He did to them. From that day forward each man forgot the speech of his friend and they no longer understood how to speak in one and the same language. So when a man said to his companion: "Give me a stone to build," he would give him mortar; and if he said: "Give me mortar," he would give him a stone. When the builder took the mortar or the stone that he had not asked for from his friend, the builder would fling them at his companion, who perished. And they did this for many a day, so that a great many of them perished because of it.

And the Lord smote the three groups who were there and taught them a lesson according to their deeds and thoughts. Those who said let us go up to heaven and serve our own gods there became apes and elephants. Those who said let us smite heaven with arrows, the Lord caused each to perish at the hands of his friends and companions. As for the third group who said let us go up to heaven and wage war against it, He dispersed them all over the earth. As for the remainder, when they understood all the ill that had befallen them, they abandoned the building and also dispersed in all directions, ceasing to build the city and the tower. That is why this place was called Babel, for there the Lord turned the speech of the whole earth into a babble. And the place lies east of the land of Shinar.

Now as for the tower which men had built, the earth opened her mouth and swallowed up the bottom third. Fire fell from heaven and burned the top third. The remaining third stands to this day and hangs open to the winds of heaven; and its shadow is a three days' journey.

Questions for Discussion

Did the people in this story sin? If so, what is their sin? Why this punishment (especially if they did not sin)?

What does the story have to say about communication between people?

Why does the narrative begin by emphasizing that everyone spoke the same language?

Does a common language necessarily bring about unity of purpose? Why is language so important in this story?

Why build a "tower with its top in the sky?"

What does "to make a name for ourselves" mean?

Why would the people become scattered if they did not build a tower? This verse presents the only reference to a motive. What was it? What was wrong with it? Can it be seen positively?

God seems to be saying that if people unify they can accomplish anything. Is God afraid, then, of the people and does he scatter them for this reason?

What does the tower represent? Is it a challenge to God or an attack on Him? Is it a pathway to heaven? If so, why would God not want the people to reach Him?

Did they approach God in the wrong manner? Was it an attempt to be like God? To dethrone God?

Was it a sincere but naive attempt to approach God? Or was this approach too easy?

Why scatter the people and also confuse their speech? Isn't one of these sufficient punishment?

Was scattering them an attempt to teach them a lesson rather than a punishment?

What would have happened if God had not stopped them? Would they have reached heaven? Overthrown God? Ceased to be human? Brought the world as we know it to an end?

Additional Study Suggestions

Compare this story with the story of the flood. What does each generation do wrong, and why is one generation punished so much more harshly than the other?

Is it dangerous to approach God even if it is done with the best of intentions? See Exodus 10:1-11 and 2 Samuel 6:1-12.

Suggested Questions for Children

What were the people doing wrong?

Why did God punish them by confusing their speech?

Do you think it would be good if everyone spoke the same language? What things would a common language make possible? What would it destroy?

We close our Shabbat study with the concluding prayer on page 40.

UNIT III

ethical living

Pirkei Avot, commonly translated as *Ethics of the Fathers,* is part of the Talmud. While the Talmud is made up of a mixture of laws, theology and legends, the *Ethics of the Fathers* consists solely of a series of sayings by various rabbis concerning the question of how to be righteous human beings.

The *Ethics of the Fathers* begins with Moses receiving the Torah at Sinai and teaching it to Joshua, who taught it to the elders, and so on down through the ages until the times of the Talmud. Thus, a claim is made that the Torah has been handed down in an unbroken chain from Sinai. It became the custom to study the *Ethics of the Fathers* between Passover and Shavuot, one chapter for each of the Shabbatot between the two holidays.

Our reading features the five outstanding disciples of Rabbi Yohanan ben Zakkai, who was the leading scholar during the period following the destruction of the Temple in 70 A.D. Given the nature of the material, each of the six selections should be individually read and discussed.

Basic Rules of Morality[9]

From the Ethics of the Fathers

2:13. He (Yohanan ben Zakkai) said to them: Go and see which is the best quality to which a man should cling. Rabbi Eliezer said: A good eye (generosity); Rabbi Joshua said: A good friend (friendliness); Rabbi Yose said: A good neighbor (goodwill); Rabbi Simeon said: One who considers the probable consequences (foresight); Rabbi Elazar said: A good heart (unselfishness). Said he to them: I prefer what Elazar ben Arakh has said to what you have said, because in his words yours are included.

15. They each said three things. Rabbi Eliezer said: Let your friend's honor be as dear to you as your own; be not easily provoked to anger; repent one day before your death (every day, for you may die tomorrow). He further said: Warm yourself by the fire of the scholars, but beware of their glowing coals (treat them respectfully), lest you burn yourself; for the bite of scholars is as hurtful as that of a fox, their sting is as deadly as that of a scorpion, their hiss is like that of a serpent, and all their words are like coals of fire (and should be heeded).

16. Rabbi Joshua said: The evil eye (greed), the evil impulse and hatred of mankind shorten a man's life.

17. Rabbi Yose said: Let your friend's property be as precious to you as your own; give yourself to studying the Torah, for it does not come to you by inheritance; and let all your deeds be done in the name of Heaven.

18. Rabbi Simeon said: Be careful in reading the Shema and the Shemoneh Esreh; when you pray, do not regard your prayer as a perfunctory act, but as a plea for mercy and grace before God, as it is said: "For he is gracious and merciful, slow to anger, abounding in kindness, and relenting of evil." Do not be wicked in your own esteem (lest you set yourself a low standard of conduct).

19. Rabbi Elazar said: Be eager to study the Torah; know what to answer an unbeliever; know before whom you toil, who your employer is, who will pay you the reward of your labor.

Questions for Discussion

2:13

What is the difference between a good eye and a good heart?

What is the difference between a good friend and a good neighbor?

Why does "one who considers the probable consequences" fit in here?

How does a good heart encompass all the rest?

What do these standards have in common? How are they different? Are these realistic goals to strive for or unattainable ideals?

Which would you have chosen, or would you have suggested some other quality?

Are the three statements in each of these groups connected or unrelated? Can some sort of world view be abstracted by taking each threesome together?

Is there any connection between these statements and what each scholar said above in 2:13?

Do you disagree with any of these statements?

Which three would you have chosen? Would you add any not included here?

15

"Let your friend's honor . . ." Compare this statement to "Love your neighbor as yourself." How do love and honor differ? How do neighbor and friend differ?

"He further said . . ." What is Rabbi Eliezer, himself a scholar, trying to say about the dangers of being in contact with the rabbis?

16

How do these things shorten a man's life?

17

"Let your friend's property . . ." Compare with 2:15: "Let your friend's honor . . ." Which is more important, property or honor?

"Give yourself to studying . . ." What are the implications of the statement "for it does not come to you by inheritance?"

18

How do the first two statements, which are concerned with prayer, relate to the last one?

What is the importance of the first statement?

Is Rabbi Simeon more concerned than the others about the individual and less about the interpersonal?

19

"Know what to answer an unbeliever . . ." Why is it important to be able to answer an unbeliever?

"Know before whom you toil . . ." Why this image?

"Know before whom you toil, who your employer is . . ." Is there a difference between him before whom you toil and your employer?

Suggested Questions for Children

If you could endow yourself with one quality, what would it be? What is the quality you admire most in other people?

Why do you think the rabbis warned against anger? Can anger be constructive as well as destructive? Is it legitimate to be angry at times?

We close our Shabbat study with the concluding prayer on page 40.

halakha-jewish law

The texts in this unit are taken from the Babylonian Talmud. The first deals with the authority of Jewish law. Since the Talmudic text may be a little difficult for people unfamiliar with it, read it together out loud, using the explanatory notes to understand the meaning. You need not understand the specific law over which the rabbis are arguing to be able to discuss the broader issues presented.

The second text, the end of the story, can be read at the same time as the first, or you can stop and discuss the first before going on to the second. The second text is the continuation of the story and tells us something about the humanity of the rabbis. It should be noted that Rabbi Joshua and Rabbi Eliezer are two of the scholars previously encountered in Unit III, the extract from the "Ethics of the Fathers."

The story begins with an argument over whether a certain oven can become impure or not. Rabbi Eliezer argues that it cannot, the rabbis argue that it can.

Eliezer ben Hyrcanus and the Rabbis: A Debate[10]

From the Babylonian Talmud

On the day R. Eliezer brought forward every imaginable argument, but they did not accept them. Said he to them: "If the halachah agrees with me, let this carob tree prove it!" Thereupon the carob-tree was torn a hundred cubits out of its place—others affirm, four hundred cubits. "No proof can be brought from a carob-tree," they retorted. Again he said to them: "If the halachah agrees with me, let the stream of water prove it!"

Whereupon the stream of water flowed backwards. "No proof can be brought from a stream of water," they rejoined. Again he urged: "If the halachah agree with me, let the walls of the schoolhouse prove it!" Whereupon the walls inclined to fall. But R. Joshua rebuked them, saying: "When scholars are engaged in a halachic dispute, what have ye to interfere?" Hence they did not fall, in honor of R. Joshua, nor did they resume the upright, in honor of R. Eliezer; and they are still standing thus inclined.

Again he said to them: "If the halachah agrees with me, let it be proved from Heaven!" Whereupon a Heavenly Voice cried out: "Why do ye dispute with R. Eliezer, seeing that in all matters the halachah agrees with him!" But R. Joshua arose and exclaimed: "It is not in heaven." What did he mean by this?—Said R. Jeremiah: That the Torah had already been given at Mount Sinai: we pay no attention to a Heavenly Voice, because Thou hast long since written in the Torah at Mount Sinai: "After the majority must one incline" (Exodus 23:2).

R. Nathan met Elijah and asked him: "What did the Holy One, Blessed be He, do in that hour?" He laughed (with joy); he replied, saying: "My sons have defeated Me, My sons have defeated Me."

It was said: On that day all objects which R. Eliezer had declared clean were brought and burnt in fire. Then they took a vote and excommunicated him. Said they, "Who shall go and inform him?" "I will go," answered R. Akiba, "lest an unsuitable person go and inform him, and thus destroy the whole world." What did R. Akiba do? He donned black garments and wrapped himself in black, and sat at a distance of four cubits from him. "Akiba," said R. Eliezer to him, "what has particularly happened today?" "Master," he replied, "it appears to me that thy companions hold aloof from thee." Thereupon he too rent his garments, put off his shoes, removed (his seat) and sat on the earth, whilst tears streamed from his eyes.

A Tanna taught: Great was the calamity that befell that day, for everything at which R. Eliezer cast his eyes was burned up. R. Gamaliel too was travelling in a ship, when a huge wave arose to drown him. "It appears to me," he reflected, "that this is on account of none other but R. Eliezer b. Hyrcanus." Thereupon he rose and exclaimed, "Sovereign of the Universe! Thou knowest full well that I have not acted for my honour, nor for the honour of my parental house, but for Thine, so that strife may not multiply in Israel!" At that the raging sea subsided.

Ima Shalom was R. Eliezer's wife, and sister to R. Gamaliel. From the time of this incident onwards she did not permit him to fall upon his face.

One day a poor man came and stood at the door, and she took out some bread to him. (On her return) she found him fallen on his face. "Arise," she cried out to him, "thou hast slain my brother." In the meanwhile an announcement was made from the house of Rabbi Gamaliel that he had died. "Whence dost thou know it?" he questioned her. "I have this tradition from my father's house: All gates are locked, excepting the gates of wounded feelings."

Eliezer ben Hyrcanus and the Rabbis: The Conclusion[11]

From the Babylonian Talmud

When R. Eliezer fell sick, R. Akiba and his companions went to visit him. The Sages entered his chamber and sat down at a distance of four cubits. "Why have ye come?" said he to them. "To study the Torah," they replied. "And why did ye not come before now?" he asked. They answered, "We had no time." He then said, "I will be surprised if these die a natural death." R. Akiba asked him, "And what will my death be?" and he answered, "Yours will be more cruel than theirs." He then put his two arms over his heart and bewailed them, saying, "Woe to you, two arms of mine, that have been like two Scrolls of the Law that are wrapped up. Much Torah have I studied, and much have I taught. Much Torah have I learnt, yet have I but skimmed from the knowledge of my teachers as much as a dog lapping from the sea. Much Torah have I taught, yet my disciples have only drawn from me as much as a painting stick from its tube. Moreover, I have studied three hundred laws on the subject of a deep bright spot, yet no man has ever asked me about them." His visitors then asked him, "What is the law of a ball, a shoemaker's last, an amulet, a leather bag containing pearls, and a small weight?" He replied, "They can become unclean, and if unclean, they are restored to their uncleanliness just as they are." Then they asked him, "What of a shoe that is on the last?" He replied, "It is clean;" and in pronouncing this word his soul departed. Then R. Joshua arose and exclaimed, "The vow is annulled, the vow is annulled!" On the conclusion of the Sabbath R. Akiba met his bier being carried from Caesarea to Lydda. (In his grief) he beat his flesh until the blood flowed down upon the earth. Then R. Akiba commenced his funeral address, the mourners being lined up about the coffin, and said: "My father, my father, the chariot of Israel and the horsemen thereof; I have many coins, but no money changer to accept them."

Explanatory Notes

"After the majority." Since Sinai, halakhic decisions have been in the hands of the rabbis, to be decided by majority vote.

"Elijah." It was believed that Elijah the prophet, who had never died, often appeared to the rabbis.

"At a distance of four cubits." You were not allowed to approach within a distance of four cubits someone who was excommunicated.

"Fall upon his face." There is a custom to fall upon your face (i.e. lay your hand upon your head) during a section of the daily service. This is a time for personal prayer.

"All gates are locked." The gates of prayer to God are locked, that is, it is difficult to get a response, except to wounded feelings.

"If these die a natural death." Rabbi Eliezer had a premonition that these rabbis would be killed. This is a reference to the martyrdom of ten leading rabbis at the hands of the Romans. This incident is traditionally recited during the *musaf* service on Yom Kippur.

"That are wrapped up." So that they cannot be read. Similarly, no one had learned from him because of the ban of excommunication.

"A deep bright spot." One of the forms of leprosy; see Leviticus 12:2.

"Law of a ball . . . a small weight." Rabbi Eliezer held the opinion that these were receptacles and therefore could become impure. The rabbis were asking Rabbi Eliezer whether he still held to this view in opposition to the rest of the rabbis.

"A shoe . . . on a last." Rabbi Eliezer maintained that a new shoe that was still on the last upon which it was made could not become impure.

"The vow is annulled." The ban of excommunication is lifted.

"But no money changer to accept them." Rabbi Akiba is saying that he has many questions about the law, but now has no one who can answer them.

Questions for Discussion

What does this story say about the authority of the halakhah—the law?

What is God's role in creating the law? What is the rabbis' role?

What does it say about the infallibility of the law if it can be decided against divine authority?

Why is what Elijah has to relate important?

Why did Rabbi Eliezer ben Hyrcanus refuse to give in? Why did the rabbis excommunicate him?

Do you think Rabbi Eliezer should have given in to the other rabbis? How do you balance the need for consensus against the rights and beliefs of individuals?

What was the relationship of the sages toward Rabbi Eliezer after the excommunication? At his death?

What was Rabbi Eliezer's feeling toward them?

Look at the statements quoted in the names of Rabbi Joshua and Rabbi Eliezer ben Hyrcanus in Unit III, above. Do these statements take on new meanings in light of the story?

Suggested Questions for Children

Do you think it is important to give in to the majority even when you know that you are right and the others are wrong? Or should you continue to oppose the majority? How can a group function unless the minority abides by the decisions of the majority? Yet, how can anyone agree to something that he believes is wrong?

What does the story tell us about having respect for people you disagree with?

We close our Shabbat study with the concluding prayer on page 40.

parents and children

The first text in this unit, from Genesis, is the story of how Isaac attempted to bless his son Esau and how he was fooled into blessing Jacob instead. It is important to point out that the blessing represented the choosing of Isaac's heir. From the Bible's point of view, it was not the material inheritance that was significant about being the heir; it was the spiritual inheritance. Whoever was blessed by Isaac would be the next link in the chain of Israel's history. This effect of the blessing should be taken into account as the story is read.

You can read the story and then discuss it, using the questions provided. Or you might assign the four characters to different persons who are to defend their roles and explain their motivations. Four others, or even the same four, could then attack the role of each of the characters. The story also lends itself to acting out through role playing.

The second text is a supplementary reading, which tries to explain Rebekah's viewpoint. It can be read after you finish discussing the story, or after you have discussed it for a period of time and would like another viewpoint on it.

The Blessing of Jacob[12]

From the Book of Genesis

When Esau was forty years old, he took to wife Judith daughter of Beeri the Hittite, and Básemath daughter of Elon the Hittite; and they were a source of bitterness to Isaac and Rebekah. When Isaac was old and his eyes were too dim to see, he called his older son Esau and said to him, "My son." He answered, "Here I am." And he said, "I am, you see, so old that I do not know how soon I may die. Take, then, your gear, your quiver and bow, and go out into the country and hunt me some game. Then make me a tasty dish such as I like, and bring it to me to eat, so that I may give you my innermost blessing before I die."

Rebekah had been listening as Isaac spoke to his son Esau. When Esau had gone out to the country to hunt game to bring home, Rebekah said to her son Jacob, "I overheard your father speaking to your brother Esau, saying, 'Bring me some game and make me a tasty dish to eat that I may bless you, with the Lord's approval, before I die.' Now, my son, listen carefully as I instruct you. Go to the flock and fetch me two choice kids, and I will make of them a tasty dish for your father, such as he likes. Then take it to your father to eat, in order that he may bless you before he dies." Jacob answered his mother Rebekah, "But my brother Esau is a hairy man and I am smooth-skinned. If my father touches me, I shall appear to him as a trickster and bring upon myself a curse, not a blessing." But his mother said to him, "Your curse, my son, be upon me! Just do as I say and go fetch them for me."

He got them and brought them to his mother, and his mother prepared a tasty dish such as his father liked. Rebekah then took the best clothes of her older son Esau, which were there in the house, and had her younger son Jacob put them on; and she covered his hands and the hairless part of his neck with the skins of the kids. Then she put in the hands of her son Jacob the tasty dish and the bread that she had prepared.

He went to his father and said, "Father." And he said, "Yes, which of my sons are you?" Jacob said to his father, "I am Esau, your first-born; I have done as you told me. Pray sit up and eat of my game, that you may give me your innermost blessing." Isaac said to his son, "How did you succeed so quickly, my son?" And he said, "Because the Lord your God granted me good fortune." Isaac said to Jacob, "Come closer that I may feel you, my son—whether you are really my son Esau or not." So Jacob drew close to his father Isaac, who said as he felt him, "The voice is the voice of Jacob, but the hands are the hands of Esau." He did not recognize him because his hands were hairy like those of his brother Esau. As he prepared to bless him, he asked, "Are you really my son Esau?" And when he said, "I am," he said, "Serve me and let me eat of my son's game that I may give you my innermost blessing." So he served him and he ate, and he brought him wine and he drank. Then his father Isaac said to him, "Come close and kiss me, my son"; and he went up and kissed him. And he smelled his clothes and he blessed him, saying,

See, the smell of my son
Is as the smell of the field
That the Lord has blessed.
May God give you
Of the dew of heaven and the fat of the earth,
Abundance of new grain and wine.
Let peoples serve you,
And nations bow to you;
Be master over your brothers,
And let your mother's sons bow to you.
Cursed be they who curse you,
Blessed they who bless you.

No sooner had Jacob left the presence of his father Isaac—after Isaac had finished blessing Jacob—than his brother Esau came back from his hunt. He too prepared a tasty dish and brought it to his father. And he said to his father, "Let my father sit up and eat of his son's game, so that you may give me your innermost blessing." His father Isaac said to him, "Who are you?" And he said, "Esau, your first-born!" Isaac was seized with very violent trembling. "Who was it then," he demanded, "that hunted game and brought it to me? Moreover, I ate of it before you came, and I blessed him; now he must remain blessed!" When Esau heard his father's words, he burst into wild and bitter sobbing, and said to his father, "Bless me too, Father!" But he answered, "Your brother came with guile and took away your blessing." [Esau] said, "Was he then named Jacob that he might supplant me these two times? First he took away my birthright and now he has taken away my blessing!" And he added, "Have you not reserved a blessing for me?" Isaac answered, saying to Esau, "But I have made him master over you: I have given him all his brothers for servants, and sustained him with grain and wine. What, then, can I still do for you, my son?" And Esau said to his father, "Have you but one blessing, Father? Bless me too, Father!" And Esau wept aloud. And his father Isaac answered, saying to him,

"See, your abode shall enjoy the fat of the earth
And the dew of heaven above.
Yet by your sword you shall live,
And you shall serve your brother;
But when you grow restive,
You shall break his yoke from your neck."

Epilogue

Now Esau harbored a grudge against Jacob because of the blessing which his father had given him, and Esau said to himself, "Let but the mourning period of my father come, and I will kill my brother Jacob." When the words of her older son Esau were reported to Rebekah, she sent for her younger son Jacob and said to him, "Your brother Esau is consoling himself by planning to kill you. Now then, my son, listen to me. Flee at once to Haran, to my brother Laban. Stay with him a while, until your brother's fury subsides—until your brother's anger against you subsides—and he forgets what you have done to him. Then I will fetch you from there. Let me not lose you both in one day!"

Rebekah said to Isaac, "I am disgusted with my life because of the Hittite women. If Jacob marries a Hittite woman like these, from among the native women, what good will life be to me?" So Isaac sent for Jacob and blessed him. He instructed him, saying, "You shall not take a wife from among the Canaanite women. Up, go to Paddan-aram, to the house of Bethuel, your mother's father, and take a wife there from among the daughters of Laban, your mother's brother. May El Shaddai bless you, make you fertile and numerous, so that you become a community of peoples. May He grant you the blessing of Abraham, to you and your offspring; that you may possess the land where you are sojourning, which God gave to Abraham."

Then Isaac sent Jacob off, and he went to Paddan-aram, to Laban the son of Bethuel the Aramean, the brother of Rebekah, mother of Jacob and Esau.

When Esau saw that Isaac had blessed Jacob and sent him off to Paddan-aram to take a wife from there, charging him, as he blessed him, "You shall not take a wife from among the Canaanite women," and that Jacob had obeyed his father and mother and gone to Paddan-aram, Esau realized that the Canaanite women displeased his father Isaac. So Esau went to Ishmael and took to wife, in addition to the wives he had, Mahalath the daughter of Ishmael, sister of Nebaioth.

Questions for Discussion

About Isaac

Why does Isaac choose Esau? Does his character appeal to Isaac, or is it simply that Esau is the first-born, and so by right the blessing is his?

Is Isaac making the right choice?

Do you think he was fooled by Jacob?

How do you think he feels afterwards toward Rebekah? Esau? Jacob? Is there any evidence of his attitude in the text?

About Rebekah

Why does Rebekah favor Jacob? Is it Jacob's character that appeals to Rebekah, or does she dislike Esau?

Are Rebekah and Isaac just playing favorites with their children? If not, if their choices are related to each child's character, what does that say about the parents' characters?

How much does the fact that the one chosen will be the next leader of Israel signify in all this?

Can Rebekah's action be justified?

Why did she not discuss the choice with Isaac, rather than fool him?

How does Rebekah feel afterwards toward Isaac, Jacob and especially Esau?

About Jacob

Was Jacob right to listen to his mother?

How could he honor the conflicting wishes of his parents?

What should he have done?

About Esau

Is Esau a terribly wronged person?

Is there another way to read the story?

What is the significance of the beginning and the end of the story, which speaks of Esau's wives?

How do you think he feels toward his parents after the story?

About all

Who do you believe behaved worst in the story? Best? How would you have behaved if you had been Jacob? Isaac? Rebekah? Esau?

Suggested Questions for Children

Do you think it was fair for Rebekah to favor one of her children over the other? For Isaac? Is there any circumstance when a parent is justified in doing this?

If you had been Jacob, would you have obeyed your mother and fooled your father?

Rebecca's Last Words

By Michael Strassfeld

I, Rebecca, daughter of Bethuel, repent of all my sins and of hurts caused by me as I lie here feeling Death tugging at the tent pegs of my soul. May all those whom I hurt forgive me as I at this moment have forgiven them. Most of all, I wish forgiveness from my dear Isaac and our two sons, Esau and Jacob, for what I was compelled to do on that day.

Even in my womb, I felt that Jacob and Esau were struggling against each other. From their birth, the pattern was set—Esau, the stronger, emerging first; Jacob being pulled from the womb by holding onto his brother's heel. That is the way it was; perhaps that is the way it will always be.

Thus they grew up, Esau achieving his ends by force, and Jacob soon learning how to overcome his stronger brother by the use of his mind. I loved them both, but felt I must protect Jacob both from his brother and from the cruel forces of this world. Isaac was blind to Jacob's silent suffering at the hands of his brother.

I cannot comprehend how Isaac could make such a terrible mistake. Even he should have known that only Jacob could be his spiritual heir, a founder of God's nation. I still cannot understand why he chose Esau to receive his blessings. But I knew I had to act.

I would like to believe that Isaac not only knew what I was doing (for even blind he could not have been fooled by my simple stratagem) but in fact actually wanted me to substitute Jacob for Esau, to make the right choice that he could not make. I would like to believe that, but I am probably fooling myself. From that day to this, the topic is as unmentioned as that of Isaac's childhood.

And so I convinced a reluctant Jacob to fool his father in order to receive the blessing. Poor Jacob, caught between obedience to me and to his father. I wonder if he still regrets it—and regrets his exile to Laban in Paddan-aram.

And most of all Esau, my son who cannot believe that I am really his mother. He could not understand that I loved him even on that day, and still do to this day. I had to do what I did, despite my love, for the sake of that mission which has made us wanderers in this land.

And so here I lie dying, alone. This unspoken thing lies between me and Isaac; my son Esau hates me; and my son Jacob is far away I sent for him and I am sure that even now Jacob is hurrying to be at my side. I fear he will be too late.

I ask of all their forgiveness, and hope at least that I will take Esau's hate to the grave with me, so that he and Jacob can be reconciled.

God in Heaven, forgive your maidservant Rebecca.

We close our Shabbat study with the concluding prayer on page 40.

tzedakah - giving to the poor

Tzedakah is usually translated as "charity," but this gives a false sense of what the word means. "Charity" connotes aiding the poor as an act of loving-kindness; *tzedakah*, on the other hand, is from the root *tzedek*, meaning "justice," for Judaism sees the support of the poor as part of the just way to live. To give *tzedakah* is an obligation, not just a voluntary deed of good will.

The first text in this unit is from the writings of Moses Maimonides (1135–1204). Maimonides (also known as the RaMBaM, an acronym of his name *R*abbi *M*oses *b*en *M*aimon) lived in Spain and Egypt. He was the greatest Jewish philosopher of the Middle Ages, as well as an outstanding legal authority and an eminent physician. The passages chosen are from his *Mishneh Torah*, a legal code, from a section entitled *Mattanot le'aniyim*, "Gifts to the Poor." Since they are legal texts, each should be individually read and studied.

Also included is a supplementary text, a short story by the contemporary American writer Hugh Nissenson. This story tells of the tension of giving to a person who, because of his poverty, has manners and an appearance that are troubling to the giver. It deals with the meaning of *tzedakah* by focusing on the traditional theme *tzedakah tatzil mi-mavet*, "the giving of charity saves you from death." The story can be used in addition to the selection from Maimonides, though some may wish to use it instead.

Giving to the Poor[14]

By Moses Maimonides

1. You are required to sustain a poor person in accordance with what it is that he lacks. If he has no garments you are required to clothe him; if he has

no furnishings you are required to purchase them . . . Even if previously this person was accustomed to riding about on a horse with a servant running before him, and then he became impoverished, you are required to purchase a horse and a servant to run before him. For it is said, "Sufficient for his needs in that which he lacks" (Deuteronomy 15:8). However, you are required to give him only what he lacks; you are not required to make him wealthy.

2. If a poor person comes and asks for what he lacks, and you can not afford to give him that amount, give him what you can afford. How much is that? To give a fifth of your wealth (to charity) is exceptional. To give a tenth is the correct amount. To give less is stingy (literally an evil eye) . . . Even a poor person who sustains himself from charity is obliged to give charity to others.

3. If a poor person whom you do not know comes and states: "I am hungry, feed me," do not check to see if he is a fraud, but rather feed him right away. If he is naked and says: "Clothe me," then check to see if he is a fraud (before clothing him). If you know the poor person then you should clothe him as befits his status without checking on him.

4. There is no need to give a large amount to a poor person going from door to door, but give him a small amount. It is forbidden to give nothing if a poor person asks, even if you give him only a penny. If a poor person requests help and you have nothing in your possession to give him, placate him with words; it is forbidden to be angry at him or raise your voice at him in a shout, for his heart is broken and crushed.

5. A poor person who does not want to accept charity should be tricked into accepting it—by telling him it is a present or a loan. A person who does not want to give charity, or gives less than his financial status warrants, should be forced by the court even through the use of beatings until he gives a proper amount.

6. A poor person who is your relative takes precedence (in charity-giving) over everyone else. The poor of your household take precedence over those of your city. The poor of your city take precedence over other cities.

7. In every city where Jews reside, it is obligatory that they select from their midst those who will be in charge of *tzedakah*, persons who are known and trusted and who will go among the people and take from everyone what he

should be giving. These people will then distribute the money every Friday and give to the poor sufficient funds to sustain them for seven days.

8. An established person (i.e. not poor), who is travelling from city to city, loses his money and has nothing to eat. He is allowed to take from the various kinds of charity. When he returns to his home, he is not obliged to pay back the money, for during that period he was actually poor.

9. An individual owns houses, fields and vineyards (and yet needs money). If he sells them now in the rainy season, he would have to sell them cheaply; if he waits for the growing season, he would receive their full value. He is not forced to sell at the wrong time (to prevent him from becoming a charity case). Rather, he is sustained from the charity funds (until the proper sale time).

10. There are eight gradations of charity, one higher than the next. The highest level . . . is he who takes an impoverished person and gives him a gift or a loan or goes into partnership with him or finds him work in order to strengthen him to such a degree that he no longer has to request help from others . . .
A lower level than this is he who gives charity to the poor in such a way that he does not know to whom he gave and the poor person does not know from whom he received it . . .
A lower level than this is when the giver knows to whom he gave but the poor person does not know from whom he received . . .
A lower level than this is when the poor person knows from whom he received but the giver does not know (to whom he gave) . . .
A lower level than this is when the giver gives it into (the poor person's) hands before he is asked.
A lower level than this is when the giver gives after he is asked.
A lower level than this is when the giver gives less than he should, but with a kindly disposition.
A lower level than this is when the giver gives unhappily.

Questions for Discussion

Do you think it is right to provide someone with a horse and servant (or their modern equivalents)?

How do you differentiate between providing what he lacks and making him wealthy?

Is there a difference between physically and psychologically lacking something?

Why should a poor person give charity?

Doesn't that mean the poor person must be given additional money to replace what he gave away?

The *Jerusalem Talmud,* Pe'ah 8:9, 21b, relates: One day Rabbi Yohanan and Rabbi Simeon ben Lakish went to the public baths in Tiberias. A poor man asked them for charity. They said: "When we return." When they came back, they found him dead. They said: "Since we showed him no charity when he was alive, let us attend to him now that he is dead." When they were preparing him for burial, they found a purse full of silver pieces upon him. Then they remembered what Rabbi Abbahu had said: "We must show charity even to the deceivers, for if it were not for them, a man might be asked for alms by a poor man, and he might refuse and be punished." Is this a realistic way to deal with the fraudulent poor?

What about those beggars on the street who you think want money to buy liquor? Is it right to support them in their bad habits?

Can a differentiation be made between different types of poor persons, as Maimonides did? Or should a decision be made in each case?

Today, Jewish courts can no longer use force to persuade people to give charity. What should be done instead? Or, in the contemporary situation, should charity-giving be strictly voluntary?

There is also a statement that "the poor of the land of Israel take precedence over the poor of other lands" (Sifre Devarim 116). How does that fit in with the priorities listed by Maimonides?

Are the poor of Israel a priority over poor parents or the poor of your own city or country? How would you set your *tzedakah* priorities?

Is it important to organize a bureaucracy to handle charity funds? Wouldn't it be more efficient to let each individual give on his own?

Do you agree with Maimonides?

Do you agree with the gradations of charity described?

Is giving money to educational or cultural activities considered *tzedakah?*

Can part of the money you pay in income tax be considered *tzedakah?*

Suggested Questions for Children

Do you agree that a person should be supported in the style to which he is accustomed?

Do you think you should support any person who asks you for charity, no matter what he will do with the money you give him?

How would you order your priorities of charitable giving? To relatives, your neighborhood, your country, etc.? To cultural and educational programs as against life-saving programs? To Jewish as against non-Jewish causes?

Do you think children who receive allowances from parents should give *tzedakah?*

A Supplementary Text

Charity[15]

By Hugh Nissenson

My mother died in the winter of 1912 when I was twelve years old. At the time, I was living with my parents in one room of a cold-water flat on Ludlow Street on Manhattan's Lower East Side. My father was a finisher of men's pants. He lined the pants at the waistline and hemmed the pockets. Working twelve hours a day on his rented Singer sewing machine, he made an average of seven dollars a week. While I went to school, my mother helped him by sewing on buttons and buckles. After school, my job was to deliver bundles of the finished pants to the subcontractor on Stanton Street who had hired us.

All told, we cleared a little over ten dollars a week. We paid fourteen dollars a month rent and ate very little: a roll and a cup of chicory-flavored coffee for breakfast, a bowl of chicken soup for lunch, and a crust of rye bread and big green pickles for supper. I always went to bed hungry. The only time we splurged on food was on Friday nights in celebration of the coming of the Sabbath. As a religious Jew, my father insisted upon it. We scrimped and saved all week and on Friday afternoons my mother went shopping on Hester Street, where she bought everything from the pushcart peddlers or the outdoor stalls. Beginning Friday morning, my mouth would actually water in anticipation.

When I got home, the table—the only one we owned—would already be set with a pair of brass candlesticks and chipped china plates with little rosebuds painted on them. There would be a fresh loaf of challah, covered by a threadbare embroidered doily, a little glass goblet of sweet red wine for each of us, a plate of stuffed carp, sweet-and-sour meat, roast potatoes saturated with gravy, and candied carrots. Soup—chicken soup again—made from legs and wings, always came last, and for dessert my mother would serve calf's-foot jelly which she had cooked that afternoon and set out on the fire escape to cool. Mother would light the candles, pronounce the benediction over them, and after blessing the bread and wine, my father would turn to our guest with a nod and invite him to begin eating.

We always had a guest on Friday nights, someone even poorer than we, and alone, who had no place to go to celebrate the Sabbath. It was a religious obligation my father had brought with him from Russia. On Friday afternoons, he would take an hour off from work to wander the streets of the neighborhood, looking for a Jewish beggar or a starving Hebrew scholar who slept on the benches of some shul. They were almost always old men smelling of snuff, who wore ragged beards, earlocks, and had dirty fingernails.

They would wash their hands in the sink, mumble their prayers, and, smacking their wrinkled lips, begin to eat, making grunting noises deep in their throats. Very often, on particularly cold nights, my father would invite them to remain with us, and they would curl up on the table, covered by a woolen blanket. Their snoring made it impossible for me to sleep.

"Papa," I'd complain.

"Shhh!" he'd tell me. "Remember. 'Charity saves from death.'"

He quoted the words from the Bible in Hebrew in a resonant voice that never failed to shut me up. I would lie awake in the dark, listening to the mingled sounds of the snoring, the wheezing and occasional cough, along with the scurrying of mice across the floor. The room was freezing. Coal was too expensive to keep the stove burning all night. Very often, in the mornings, the glass of water by my bed would be frozen solid.

Then, quite suddenly, in the middle of December, my mother caught pneumonia. She awoke on a Wednesday, as I remember, about midnight, with a splitting headache and a severe chill that made her teeth chatter and a raging fever that for some reason flushed only the left side of her face. It looked as if she had been slapped. Every bone in her body ached, she complained, and within a few hours, at about two in the morning, she was suffering from an agonizing pain in her right side.

"Like a knife," she whispered through clenched teeth.

Convulsed by a short, dry cough, she lay in bed for two more days. The left side of her face was still flushed. She breathed very quickly, with a grunt every time she exhaled. When she drew a breath, her nostrils were distended. There were open sores on her upper lip. Her dark brown eyes were peculiarly bright—I had never seen them so beautiful. I wanted to kiss the quivering lips. But the barking cough made her raise herself up and claw at her right side. She began to spit blood.

In her semi-delirium, she babbled half-remembered legends from her childhood, and things she had read in Yiddish chapbooks written for women.

"Is it snowing?" she asked me.

"Yes."

"Ah, but not there," she whispered. "Never there."

"Where?" my father asked her, and she gazed at him with her glittering eyes, and smiled. "Where do you think? Where there are fruit trees, trees with golden leaves, always in bloom. Apple trees and orange trees, and one huge tree, they say, where apples, oranges, pears, and grapes grow on the same branches, all together . . ."

He rubbed her moist, hot hands. "Listen to me. This kind of talk is forbidden. Forbidden, Malka, do you understand me? Can you hear me? It's absolutely forbidden to talk this way. One must want to live."

"I've been a good wife, haven't I?" she asked.

"Of course."

"I've tried. God knows, I've tried to be a good wife, a good mother, and a good Jew."

"Of course you have," my father said.

"I'm glad. I've read, you know, that when a righteous soul is about to enter Paradise, the angels come and strip off her shroud and dress her in seven robes woven from the clouds of glory. Did you know that? Seven shining robes. And on her head they put two crowns. One of gold and the other . . . I forget now what the other is . . ."

"Stop it!" my father yelled.

"I remember," she said. "Pearls. A crown of pearls . . ."

When I came home that Friday afternoon, a doctor was there from the hospital on Second Avenue and Seventeenth Street. He was a tall German Jew who wore a blond goatee.

"Yes," he said in English, putting away his stethoscope. "The crisis will come in a week, maybe a little less."

"The crisis?" I repeated. "What's that?"

And looking down at me, he stroked his goatee. "A crisis is a crisis, my boy. It's as simple as that. She'll continue to get worse until the crisis, and then, if she's strong enough, her fever will drop and she'll survive. Of course, she'd have a much better chance in the hospital."

"What's that?" my father asked in Yiddish. "What's he saying?"

"It's up to you," the doctor went on, addressing me. "But that's my considered professional opinion."

"A hospital?" my father suddenly repeated in English. It was probably the only word he had understood. He shook his head. "No . . ." His eyes filled with tears. I knew what he was thinking. In the shtetl north of Odessa from which he'd come, the hospital was a shack on the edge of town, supported by the local burial society, where the poor were sent to die.

My mother coughed, the doctor glanced at the face of a gold watch he wore suspended from a gold chain on his vest, and said, "Well?"

"This is America, Papa," I told him. "The doctor says that Mama will have a much better chance in the hospital."

The watch ticked, my mother gasped for breath, and my father finally nodded his head.

"Good," the doctor said. "I'll make the arrangements. The ambulance will be here in about an hour. In the meantime, keep her as warm as possible."

And when I had wrapped my mother in my own quilt, stuffed with goose feathers, my father said, "God forgive me. I almost forgot."

"What?"

"You'll have to do the shopping," he told me.

"For what?"

"For the Sabbath, what do you think?"

"Tonight?"

"The Sabbath is the Sabbath."

"I'm not hungry tonight."

"But our guest will be."

"Tonight?" I repeated.

"And why should tonight be different from last Friday night, or the Friday before that?"

My mother coughed again into her handkerchief. When she brought it away from her mouth, it was soaked with blood.

"Listen to your father," she whispered.

"No."

"Do what he tells you," she said.

I went down to Hester Street. In spite of the bitter cold and the grimy slush in which the horse-drawn wagons had made ruts, it was jammed with shoppers. For a moment, I stopped in front of a pushcart peddler who was selling cracked eggs at a penny apiece. Then, all at once, I understood. It was a *mitzvah* my father was performing, a good deed, a holy act, which bound together the upper and nether worlds, and hastened the redemption of Israel. I glanced up at the low clouds, hanging just above the city, which had a reddish glow, reflecting the lights below. It was a sign; the heavens and the earth had come closer together. And tonight of all nights, when it was a matter of life and death. The Holy One, blessed be He, saw everything. My father's charity would not go unrewarded. I walked on through the slush that seeped into my shoes. Scrawny chickens and half-plucked geese hung by their feet in a doorway and, still fluttering, awaited the butcher's knife. The butcher himself, his brawny arms covered with feathers and spattered with blood, chewed on a black cigar, spat into the gutter, and tested the blade of his knife on the ball of his thumb. It began to snow.

By the time I reached home, my mother was gone, but there with my father was a tall, emaciated, stoop-shouldered man wearing a ragged black frock coat and a battered black silk top hat. Over one arm, he carried an umbrella.

"This is Reb Rifkin," said my father.

"I know. *Shabbat shalom.*"

"And a peaceful Sabbath to you, too," Rifkin answered me in his high, cracked voice.

I had seen him around the neighborhood for years. He was a broken-down Hebrew teacher who barely kept himself alive by giving Hebrew lessons for ten cents apiece. He lived in a shul on Essex Street, where he slept in a tiny unheated room behind the Ark. It was said that rats had once attacked him and bitten off part of one of his toes.

Shivering, he warmed his blue hands over the coal stove while my father and I prepared supper. Because the doctor had been so expensive—two dollars—we had only a little chicken soup with noodles, half a loaf of stale challah, the head of a carp, a bowlful of raisins and almonds for dessert, and a glass of steaming tea with lemon. My father gave Rifkin the fish head and he devoured everything except the eyes and the bones, which he sucked one by one.

"God bless you," he said, wiping his fingers on his beard. "Would you believe it? Except for a little salted herring and a glass of tea, this is the only thing I've had in my mouth for six days. As God is my witness. Six whole days."

A little color had already seeped into his thin face with its greenish complexion. He had a tiny white spot on his right pupil which made him seem unable to look you straight in the eye. He appeared to gaze slightly above you and a little to the left.

"How's Mama?" I asked my father.

"In God's hands."

"How true. Aren't we all?" asked Rifkin. "If I hadn't gone for a walk on

Ludlow Street and met you, I'd be in my room right now, lying in the dark. Do you know that the rats there eat my candles?''

"When can we visit her?" I went on.

"Tomorrow."

"I heard the sad news," Rifkin said to me. "But don't you worry about a thing. God willing, she'll be well in no time."

"I hope so," my father said.

"How can you doubt it?" Rifkin cried out. "God is just, but He's merciful too. To whom will He not show His mercy if not to a fine woman like that and her husband who feeds the starving?"

"We shall see," my father said.

"Well, I should be going," said Rifkin, picking up his umbrella.

"Nonsense," my father said. "It's snowing. You'll stay the night and share breakfast with us tomorrow morning. Lunch and supper too, if you like. Whatever we have in the house."

"No, no, I couldn't think of it."

"But I insist."

"Well, of course, if you put it like that . . ."

As I had expected, Rifkin snored; not only snored, but whistled. I couldn't sleep, so I got up and with the blanket wrapped around my shoulders went out onto the landing. We lived on the fourth floor. The building reeked of urine from the toilets at the end of each hallway and the smell of cooked cabbage, fried onions, and fish. There was the whir of sewing machines. To make ends meet, God help us, some Jews were forced to work on the Sabbath. I sat down on the steps. The words of the proverb rang in my head: ". . . but he that hath mercy on the poor, happy is he."

"Jacob, is that you?" my father whispered when I went back into the room.

"Yes, Papa."

"Are you all right?"

"Fine, Papa."

"Come over here a minute."

"What's the matter?"

"I can't sleep."

"Neither could I, but I feel much better now."

"Do you? Why?"

"Because Mama will get well."

"How can you be so sure?"

"You said so yourself."

"Did I? When?"

"You said that charity saves from death."

"What's that got to do with Mama?"

"Everything."

He suddenly raised his voice. "Is that what you think a *mitzvah* is? A bribe offered the Almighty?"

"But you said so. You said that charity saves from death," I insisted.

Rifkin, half awakened, turned over and groaned.

"No, not Mama," my father said in a hoarse voice. "Him."

We close our Shabbat study with the concluding prayer on page 40.

UNIT VII

the spiritual versus the material

This unit centers on a story retold in Abraham Joshua Heschel's *The Sabbath*. His version is based on those found in the Babylonian Talmud and in the *Maaseh Book*, a medieval collection of stories and legends.

Heschel (1907–1972) was a leading Jewish scholar, philosopher and political activist. His best known books are: *Man is not Alone, God in Search of Man*, and *The Prophets*.

As supplementary material we have included Heschel's interpretation of the story. This should be looked at only after you have discussed the story.

The Splendor of Space[16]

An Allegorical Interpretation of an Ancient Debate
By Abraham Joshua Heschel

The time: about the year 130.
The place: Palestine.
The people present: Three leading scholars and one outsider. The place and the people under the dominion of the Roman Empire.

Rabbi Judah ben Ilai, Rabbi Jose, and Rabbi Shimeon ben Yohai were sitting together, and with them was a man called Judah ben Gerim. Rabbi Judah opened the discussion and said:

—How fine are the works of this people (the Romans)! They have made roads and market places, they have built bridges, they have erected bathhouses.

Rabbi Jose was silent.

Then Rabbi Shimeon ben Yohai replied and said:

—All that they made they made for themselves. They made roads and market places to put harlots there; they built bridges to levy tolls for them; they erected bathhouses to delight their bodies.

Judah ben Gerim went home and related to his father and mother all that had been said. And the report of it spread until it reached the government. Decreed the government:

—Judah who exalted us shall be exalted; Jose who was silent shall go into exile; Shimeon who reviled our work shall be put to death.

When Rabbi Shimeon heard of the decree, he took his son Rabbi Eleazar with him and hid in the House of Learning. And his wife came every day and brought him stealthily bread and a jug of water. When Rabbi Shimeon heard that men were searching for them and trying to capture them, he said to his son:

—We cannot rely upon a woman's discretion. . . . She may be tortured until she discloses our place of concealment.

So they went together into the field and hid themselves in a cave, so that no man knew what had become of them. And a miracle happened: a carob tree grew up inside the cave and a well of water opened, so that they had enough to eat and enough to drink. They took off their clothes and sat up to their necks in sand. The whole day they studied Torah. And when the time for prayer came, they put their clothes on and prayed, and then they put them off and again dug themselves into the sand, so that their clothes should not wear away. Thus they spent twelve years in the cave.

When the twelve years had come to an end, Elijah the prophet came and, standing at the entrance of the cave, exclaimed:

—Who will inform the son of Yohai that the emperor is dead and his decree has been annulled?

When they heard this, they emerged from the cave. Seeing the people plowing the fields and sowing the seed, they exclaimed:

—These people forsake eternal life and are engaged in temporary life!

Whatever they looked upon was immediately consumed by the fire of their eyes. Thereupon a voice from heaven exclaimed:

—Have ye emerged to destroy My world? Return to your cave!

So they returned and dwelled there another twelve months; for, they said, the punishment of the wicked in hell lasts only twelve months.

When the twelve months had come to an end, the voice was heard from heaven saying:

—Go forth from your cave!

Thus they went out. Wherever Rabbi Eleazar hurt, Rabbi Shimeon healed. Said Rabbi Shimeon:

—My son, if only we two remain to study the Torah, that will be sufficient for the world.

It was the eve of the Sabbath when they left the cave, and as they came out they saw an old man carrying two bundles of myrtle in his hand, a sweet-smelling herb having the perfume of paradise.

—What are these for, they asked him.

—They are in the honor of the Sabbath, the old man replied.

Said Rabbi Shimeon to his son:

—Behold and see how dear God's commands are to Israel . . .

At that moment they both found tranquility of soul.

Questions for Discussion

What is the nature of the argument about the Romans? Is Shimeon ben Yohai right about the Romans' motivations? Even so, what is wrong with their building things for their own use?

What is the symbolism of:

> hiding in the house of learning
> the cave
> the carob tree and the well of water
> taking off and putting on clothes
> studying while up to the neck in sand
> the number twelve
> Elijah
> the old man
> the myrtles?

Why, upon emerging from the cave, were Shimeon and Eleazar angry? Were they right? What happened during the additional twelve months spent in the cave that caused the father's, but not the son's, attitude to change?

Why does Shimeon say: "If only we two remain to study the Torah, that will be sufficient for the world"?

Why does meeting the old man bring them tranquility? Was not Shimeon already reconciled?

What does Shabbat have to do with all this?

How had the argument about Rome developed during the story? Is there a link between that argument, the feelings of the two about people plowing, and Shabbat at the end of the story?

Suggested Questions for Children

Was hiding from the Romans the courageous thing to do? The correct thing to do?

If you were alone with someone in a cave for twelve years, how would you spend your time? If you could only take three things along with you, what would they be?

Do you think it was fair of Shimeon and Eleazar to be angry with those people who went on working at their jobs while the two of them were in the cave?

A Supplementary Text

Holiness in Time[17]

By Abraham Joshua Heschel

There is a mass of cryptic meaning in this silent, solitary story of one who, outraged by the scandal of desecrated time, refused to celebrate the splendor of civilized space. It symbolically describes how Rabbi Shimeon ben Yohai and his son went from exasperation and disgust with this world, which resulted in their actually trying to destroy those who were engaged in worldly activities, to a reconciliation with this world. What stirred these men was not, as it is usually understood by historians, mere patriotic resentment against the power that had vanquished and persecuted the people of Judea. From the development of the story, it becomes obvious that from the outset the issue was not only the Roman rule but also the Roman civilization. After they had spent twelve years in the cave, the scope of the issue expanded even further. It was not any more a particular civilization but all civilization, the worth of worldly living that became the problem.

Rome, in that period, was at the height of her glory. She was the mistress of the world. All the Mediterranean countries lay at her feet . . . In all her provinces, signs of immense progress in administration, engineering and the art of construction were widely visible. It was the ambition of her rulers to express the splendor of their age by adorning with public monuments every province of the empire . . .

Rome herself towered in her glory as the city on which "the looks of men and gods were turned" . . . The Colosseum with its overwhelming massiveness, the Pantheon with its lofty vaulting, and particularly the Forum of Trajan, a building of unparalleled magnificence and "admired even by the gods," seemed to proclaim that the Empire and eternity were one. The ancient man was inclined to believe that monuments will last for ever. It was, therefore, fit to bestow the most precious epithet on Rome and to call it: *the Eternal City*. The state became an object of worship, a divinity; and the Emperor embodied its divinity as he embodied its sovereignty.

It was hard not to be impressed by the triumphs of that great Empire and to disagree with the mild and gentle Rabbi Judah ben Ilai who acknowledged the boon it had brought to many lands . . . And yet, to Rabbi Shimeon ben Yohai these triumphs were shocking, hateful and repulsive. He disparaged the calculating, utilitarian spirit of Roman civilization. He knew that all these splendid edifices and public institutions were not built by the Romans to aid the people but to serve their own nefarious designs . . .

When Rabbi Shimeon ben Yohai abandoned the world of civilization to spend many years in a cave, sitting up to his neck in sand, he forfeited worldly life to attain "eternal life." Yet this was an attainment which was hardly meaningful to his persecutors. To most Romans eternity was almost a worldly concept. The survival of the soul consisted not in being carried away to a superterrestrial and blessed existence. Immortality meant either fame or the cleaving to one's home, to one's earthly abode even after death. But Rabbi Shimeon abandoned home as well as the road to fame which is usually attained by one's being active in the affairs of the world. He fled from the world where *eternity was the attribute of a city* and went to the cave where he found a way to endow life with a quality of eternity . . .

The rewards that most people won were of little worth to Rabbi Shimeon ben Yohai. He was not captivated by the things of the earth, by all the world that is bound to decay. Or was the fame one attained among men to be considered eternal? What is the worth of being remembered by men?

All flesh is grass, all the goodliness thereof is as the flower of the field . . .
The grass withereth, the flower fadeth; but the word of our God shall stand forever.

The world is transitory, but that by which the world was created—the word of God—is everlasting. Eternity is attained by dedicating one's life to the word of God, to the study of Torah . . .

To Rabbi Shimeon eternity was not attained by those who bartered time for space but by those who knew how to fill their time with spirit. To him the great problem was *time* rather than *space*; the task was how to convert time into eternity rather than how to fill space with buildings, bridges and roads; and the solution of the problem lay in study and prayer rather than in geometry and engineering . . .

It was not until Rabbi Shimeon and his son came out of the cave at the end of their second period of retreat that their minds were reconciled to the idea that the world this side of heaven is worth working in. What caused the change of mind?

It was the "old man"—symbolizing the people of Israel—who went out to meet the Sabbath with myrtles in his hand as if the Sabbath were *a bride*.

The myrtle was, in ancient times, the symbol of love, the plant of the bride. When going out to invite his friends to the wedding, the groom would carry myrtle sprigs in his hands . . . The "old man" who was running at twilight to welcome the Sabbath, holding two bundles of myrtle in his hands, personified the idea of Israel welcoming the Sabbath as a bride.

To the Romans technical civilization was the highest goal, and time for the sake of space. To Rabbi Shimeon spiritual life was the highest goal, and time for the sake of eternity. His conclusive comfort was: in spite of all dedication to temporal things, there was a destiny that would save the people of Israel, a commitment deeper than all interests—the commitment to the Sabbath.

This, then, is the answer to the problem of civilization: not to flee from the realm of space; to work with things of space but to be in love with eternity. Things are our tools; eternity, the Sabbath, is our mate. Israel is engaged to eternity. Even if they dedicate six days of the week to worldly pursuits, their soul is claimed by the seventh day.

We close our Shabbat study with the concluding prayer on page 40.

UNIT VIII

a life for a life

This unit deals with the difficult moral decisions involved in questions of life and death. The first three cases are taken from rabbinic material. The last is an account from *Holocaust and Halakhah* by Rabbi Irving Rosenbaum. Each case should be studied and discussed individually and then compared to the next.

Excerpts from Talmudic Literature

1. A certain man came to Rava and said to him: "The governor of my town has ordered me to kill someone and has warned me that if I do not do so he will have me killed (what am I to do?)." Rava replied: "Let yourself be killed but do not kill him. How do you know that your blood is redder? Perhaps the blood of the man is redder."

A company of men is confronted by non-Jews. They say, "Give us one of your number whom we will kill. If you do not, we will kill all of you!" Even though all of them will be killed, let them not deliver a single Jewish soul into their hands. However, if they specified a single individual, as for example in the case of Sheva ben Bikhri (II Samuel, chapter 20), then they may deliver him up and not themselves be killed. Rabbi Simeon ben Lakish said, "This is so only when that person is guilty of a capital offense, as was Shiva ben Bikhri." Rabbi Yohanan, however, said, "He may be delivered up, even though he is not guilty of a capital offense." (Babylonian Talmud, Tractate Pesahim, 25b.)

2. Ulla ben Kosher was wanted by the Government. He fled to Rabbi Joshua ben Levi in Lod. Messengers were sent after him. Rabbi Joshua ben

Levi entered in an argument and appeased him and said to him: It is better that a man (meaning: you, Ulla) should be slain, and that the community should not be punished on your account. He was reconciled, and Rabbi Joshua handed him over.

It had been Elijah the prophet's custom to visit Rabbi Joshua ben Levi every day. When Rabbi Joshua performed his act, Elijah stopped coming. For thirty days he fasted, and then Elijah suddenly appeared. "Why have you stayed away?" asked the Rabbi. Elijah responded: "Am I an associate of betrayers?" But he said: "Is there not a precise teaching (to support me)—about a company of men, etc.?" Elijah answered: "Is this a teaching of the Hasidim? This thing is of a nature that it should have been done by others, and not by you." (Bereshit Rabbah 74, Tosefta Terumot 73.)

3. "That thy brother may live with thee" (Leviticus 25:36). The following was expounded by Ben Petura. Two men are traveling through the desert and one of them has a flask of water. If he alone will drink the water he will reach the town but if both of them drink they will both die. Ben Petura expounded the verse "That thy brother may live with thee" to mean that both should drink and die (rather than that one should live while the other dies). But Rabbi Akiva said to him: "'That thy brother may live with thee' means that your life takes precedence over the life of your friend." (Siphra on Leviticus 25:36.)

Holocaust and Halakhah[18]

By Irving Rosenbaum

On the fifteenth of September, 1941, toward evening, Kaminski [a Nazi officer] came to the office of the *Aeltestenrat* and handed over a written order from the *Gebiets-Kommissar* of Kovno together with five thousand white certificates. On each certificate there was printed in German: "Certificate of Jewish Artisans. *Gebiets-Kommissar* of Kovno. Signed, Jordan, *Hauptsturmführer* S.A."

The order of the *Gebiets-Kommissar* directed the *Aeltestenrat* to complete the distribution of the documents to the artisans of the ghetto and their families in one day—the sixteenth of September. When Kaminski was asked what the meaning of these documents was, he answered that there would be extra rations for those receiving them, and that the general economic conditions in the ghetto would be much improved.

The next morning the *Aeltestenrat* began to distribute the certificates through a special committee of its labor office in accordance with the instructions it had received from Kaminski. Even though the entire matter raised many suspicions, they did not at first perceive any indication of impending destruction. In the early hours the distribution of the certificates proceeded in an orderly fashion and with relative calm. To be sure it was difficult to determine who was really an artisan, because many who had no experience at all had registered as skilled workers in the lists of the *Aeltestenrat*. Moreover, it was difficult to determine the actual number of family members of each artisan. Nonetheless, attempts were made to overcome these problems. The situation changed completely after noon, when the *Aeltestenrat* began to receive written requests from the German supervisors of establishments in the city in which Jewish workers from the ghetto were employed to give "their Jews" a number of "life-permits" [*Lebensscheine*]. Immediately the true meaning of the white certificates was understood and the reason for the German directive for their distribution. It was clear that the Germans had decided to allow to remain alive only five thousand Jews of the entire ghetto—those workers and their families who could be of use to them. The remaining twenty-four thousand were to be destroyed. Then the Jews understood what Kaminski had meant when he said, "the economic conditions in the ghetto would be much improved."

The news spread like lightning throughout the ghetto, which in any event was in a terrible state of tension and nervousness. By the thousands, men stormed the offices of the *Aeltestenrat* demanding to receive the white cards . . . Thousands of fear-crazed men and women pleaded, screamed, threatened, fought amongst themselves and cursed those who had distributed the cards. It is not difficult to understand the feelings of those who had had placed upon themselves the bitter responsibility of distributing the certificates—that is, determining who should live and who should die. Who was the man wise and discerning enough to find the fitting and proper criterion according to which one person merits remaining alive and another does not? . . . According to the order, the certificates were to be distributed only among the artisans and workers. Was it possible to reconcile oneself to the destruction of all other classes, including all the intellectuals? At every moment fearful and tragic questions of conscience arose which it was impossible to answer. Should one give a certificate to every member of a family—or only to one, or two, or three? To women, to children, to chronically ill people?

In the *Aeltestenrat* a radical proposal was made: To return all the "Jordan certificates" to the Germans and to let them know that the *Aeltestenrat* saw no possibility of distributing them. There were those who went further and suggested that all the white certificates should be burned. Those who made these proposals maintained that if the decree had gone forth to destroy the Jews of Kovno, it was not morally justifiable to say that a sixth of them should be singled out and spared because they were of some use to the Germans. If we were destined to be destroyed, let us all be destroyed together. It became known in the ghetto that the *Aeltestenrat* was considering these proposals, and many artisans and workers began to protest sharply and vigorously, "What right do you have to deny us and our families the right to remain alive?" They demanded that they be given the certificates which they "had coming." Moreover, some of the ghetto workers had already received certificates in the early distribution as a result of the requests of their German employers. After long and wearying discussions, the *Aeltestenrat* came to the opinion that it had no moral right to consign to destruction the five thousand Jews whom it was possible to save at this time. The *Aeltestenrat* decided, however, that it would distribute some of the certificates to persons other than workers and take upon itself the responsibility for so doing . . .

On the sixteenth of September, it was not possible to complete the distribution of the white cards. . . . So on the seventeenth, by six o'clock in the morning, violent masses of ghetto residents surrounded the *Aeltestenrat* offices, demanding the certificates. . . . In the early hours of the morning, the *Aeltestenrat* lost control of the situation. The climax came when the news spread that the Germans had set up machine guns around the ghetto and that German troops and Lithuanian partisans had already entered the ghetto and that the *Aktion* had begun. At that point, Jews began to grab hold of the white certificates and pull them out of the hands of the members of the *Aeltestenrat* and its workers, and in a matter of moments, there were none left. But the disappointed masses, the majority of whom were left without certificates, refused to believe that they were all gone. They broke into all the offices screaming hysterically; they shattered desks and files and broke windows. The chairman of the *Aeltestenrat*, Dr. Elkes, suffered a heart attack and fell unconscious. Another member of the *Aeltestenrat*, Goldberg, was pushed to the floor by the mob and did not recover consciousness for some time . . .

Explanatory Notes

1. "Your blood is redder . . ." That is, how do you know that your life is more valuable than his?

2. "Sheva ben Bikhri." He was a rebel against King David. When Joab, David's general, threatened to destroy the city where Sheva was hiding, the inhabitants killed Sheva and thus placated Joab (2 Samuel 20:1–22).

3. "Hasidim." This is a reference to the very pious, not to the modern religious movement of that name.

Questions for Discussion

What is the difference between the first and the second case?

In the second case, do you think Rabbi Joshua acted incorrectly? Would it have been right to leave such a deed to others?

Why, according to Rabbi Akiva, does the third case differ from the first?

How would you have acted in each case?

Are there any general principles you can extract from these cases?

Do you agree with them?

Suggested Questions for Children

What do you think the Council of Jewish Elders should have done with the cards once they understood what they meant?

If the cards were to be given out, who should have priority?

Do you understand the panic that people felt? Would you have felt and acted the same way?

We close our Shabbat study with the concluding prayer on page 40.

88

UNIT IX

bringing redemption
to an unredeemed world

This unit focuses on the concept of the Messiah, but also, more broadly, on the difficulty of doing good deeds in an unredeemed world. The text is the legend of how Joseph della Reyna stormed heaven, which exists in a number of versions. This version is taken from *A Treasury of Jewish Folklore*, edited by Nathan Ausubel. There is speculation that Joseph della Reyna was a real person, who lived in the 16th century.

A number of Hebrew terms are used in the story. They are translated in the Explanatory Notes following the text.

Joseph della Reyna Storms Heaven[19]

A Jewish Folk Tale

Seeing that there were in Jerusalem so many pious men who sought God and loved truth, Rabbi Joseph della Reyna came to a firm decision:

"It is high time to force the coming of the Messiah!"

He knew full well that it would not be an easy thing to accomplish. None the less, he remained hopeful that where others had failed he would succeed.

Among his disciples there were five who were pure in heart and in intention. They were cabalists who had delved deeply into the secret truths of the *Zohar*. Night and day they sat with Rabbi Joseph over their sacred studies. It was to them that he revealed all the hidden wisdom of this world and the next. Together they would grieve and lament over the Exile of the *Shekhina* and over the sorrows of the Jewish people in dispersion.

Once, as they sat studying the Cabala with deep inner rapture, Rabbi Joseph paused and said to the five disciples, "Know, that I have given much thought about you and have gone through great inner searching about myself. The Lord has blessed us with wisdom and knowledge. We have acquired a greater mastery of the Cabala than have all those who have come before us. To us have been revealed all the innermost secrets of the Torah. By its power we are capable of performing the greatest wonders. For these reasons I have come to the conclusion that it is our duty to use these exceptional powers for great ends. We are able to accomplish something that will be sure to create a tremendous stir on earth and in heaven.

"My beloved sons, it is our sacred duty to drive all evil from the world, to hasten the coming of the Messiah, to redeem the Jewish people and to bring back the Holy *Shekhina* from its long Exile.

"Don't think I have arrived at my decision lightly. I have concerned myself with this matter for a long time and have drawn up my plans in detail. But because it is difficult for one individual to accomplish such a tremendous task I therefore require your help."

The five disciples answered as with one voice, "Holy Rabbi! We are eager to do everything necessary in order to help you in this great work. We know that God, blessed be His Name, is with you, and we hope that you will succeed in achieving your goal."

When Rabbi Joseph della Reyna heard this he rejoiced greatly and said to them, "We must now make ready for our holy task. Go, therefore, and bathe, put on clean raiment, and for three days and three nights thereafter you must keep your bodies and souls pure and holy. After that you will prepare food and drink to last a long time. On the third day we will go forth into the wilderness. We cannot return until we have successfully carried out our mission."

The disciples then went about making their preparations with great inner trembling. Their spirits, too, were filled with a sacred flame and longing to accomplish their task. So they bathed and made themselves clean. They put on white raiment and renounced all worldly interests. They preserved their bodies and their thoughts in purity and holiness. They also prepared ample provisions for the long journey.

On the third day they came to Rabbi Joseph della Reyna. When they arrived they found Rabbi Joseph in deep thought; a dazzling radiance streamed from his face. He was praying with such deep ecstasy that his soul seemed to have risen aloft from this world of sin. It soared upwards into the highest regions of Heaven.

When Rabbi Joseph saw his disciples he greeted them with the tenderness of a father.

"Come to me, my beloved disciples," he said. "You have done what I have asked of you. You are now worthy of helping me in my sacred task. God, blessed be He, will most assuredly show us the way. He will help us reach our goal by the power of His Holy Name."

"Amen!" the disciples answered fervently.

Their souls became intertwined with his and rose up from the sinful world, winging their way to the pure celestial regions.

Rabbi Joseph also had completed his preparations. Besides food and drink, he took along with him a writing quill and parchment.

"Let us go!" he said to his disciples.

And then they started out on their quest.

At last they came to Meron and prayed at the grave of Rabbi Simeon ben Yohai, the teacher of all cabalists, the author of the *Zohar*.

They spent three days and three nights there. They neither ate nor slept but delved into the mysteries of the *Zohar* and sent up flaming prayers to God.

On the third day, when dawn began to break, Rabbi Joseph suddenly ended his vigil and fell asleep. This filled his disciples with alarm. Could it be that the master's spirit was blemished with weakness? But they held their peace and did not say a word.

As Rabbi Joseph slept he dreamed that Rabbi Simeon ben Yohai and his son Eleazer came and reproved him: "How rash of you to have undertaken such a terrifying task as this! Be forewarned: you will fail miserably in your attempt! You will be beset by insuperable difficulties and dangers. You cannot emerge out of this alive and, having failed, your souls will be condemned to everlasting purgatory. However, since you are resolute in your decision, let us caution you to be discreet in your speech and in your actions, so that those evil spirits who wish to do you harm may not have any power over you."

"Almighty God, blessed be His Name, knows my pure intention," replied Rabbi Joseph. "He knows full well that what I am doing is not for my selfish ends but for the good of all the Jews and of all mankind. Therefore, He will help me achieve my goal in order that I may sanctify His Name among all the peoples of the earth."

The souls of Rabbi Simeon ben Yohai and his son Eleazer then gave their blessings to Rabbi Joseph.

"May God help and keep you wherever you may turn!" they prayed.

Rabbi Joseph awoke and told his disciples what he had dreamed. They then understood that he had fallen asleep by the Will of God, and that it was not due to weakness of spirit.

Then they arose and continued on their way.

Not far from Tiberias they came to a large forest and remained there all day. They tasted neither food nor drink for they wished to purify their bodies and spirits from earthly taint.

The beauty of the forest enveloped them. Cool green trees wafted their fragrance everywhere. The birds sat in the branches trilling their songs of joy to the Creator. But Rabbi Joseph and his disciples neither saw nor heard them out of fear that sensuous thoughts might snare them away from their sacred mission.

All day long they delved into the profoundest mysteries of Cabala, studied the sacred formulae, calculated *gematriot* and drew mystic designs of God's ten emanations, the *Sefirot*.

This they did for two days and neither ate nor drank, all the time remaining apart from the earth and from its pleasures. Thirty-three times a day they purified their bodies in the Sea of Galilee and each time they repeated the holy formulae and incantations.

At the end of each day they broke their fast. But they tasted neither fish nor flesh. They ate only bread and water, but not too much of that, only enough to keep alive.

On the afternoon of the third day Rabbi Joseph and his disciples recited the *Mincha* prayers with great fervor and, as they stood silently pronouncing the eighteen benedictions, their thoughts dwelled with utmost concentration on the secret mysteries of the Cabala.

Rabbi Joseph della Reyna then prayed by himself. He invoked all the angels and seraphim to come to his aid. By the power of the Cabala he invoked the Prophet Elijah to make his appearance before him.

"O Elijah," he exhorted. "Come to me and teach me how I should behave so that I may carry through the plan I have undertaken!"

No sooner had he finished praying than Elijah appeared.

"Tell me what it is you wish and I will teach it to you," he promised.

"Forgive me, Holy Prophet, for troubling you," Rabbi Joseph replied. "Believe me, it is not for my own glory and not for that of my ancestors but for the glory of God, blessed be His Name, and of His people and of His Holy Torah. I believe I deserve your help. Show me the way I can triumph over Satan and his hosts. Show me how I can make holiness triumph over evil and thus bring redemption to all mankind."

Elijah the Prophet grew sad.

"I wish to warn you," he said, "that you have taken upon yourself a task that no human being can accomplish. In order to vanquish Satan and his demons you and your disciples must become holier and purer than you are. I might say that to triumph over Satan you will have to become like the very angels. Your aim, of course, is an exalted one and, should you succeed, you will be the happiest man on earth for you will have brought redemption to the whole world. Nevertheless, I warn you that you are attempting something beyond your human strength. Take my advice—abandon your plan!"

Thereupon Rabbi Joseph began to weep.

"Dear Prophet of God," he pleaded. "How can I give up what I have started? Do not abandon me now! It is too late for me to turn back. I have sworn before God that I will not rest until I have driven Satan from the earth and have brought Messiah, the Redeemer of the Jewish people and of all peoples. I will not rest until I have restored the *Shekhina* to the glory it possessed when the Temple still stood in Jerusalem. For these ends I am eager to sacrifice my life. Know that I will not let you go until you help me and show me the right path to follow and the right course to take."

As the Prophet Elijah looked upon Rabbi Joseph della Reyna he was filled with a great compassion for him.

"Dry your tears, dear son," he said. "I will help you in whatever way I can to fulfill your task. You and your disciples must continue fasting for twenty-one days, nor must you touch any impure thing. When you break your fast at night eat only a morsel of bread, just enough to keep alive. In addition, you must bathe twenty-one times in the Sea of Galilee so that you become pure and holy like the angels. And, when the twenty-one days are up, you must enter into a fast which will last three days and three nights. At the end of the third day you must recite the *Mincha* prayers wearing *talith* and *tefillin*. After that you must recite the verse: 'Flaming angels surround the Holy One, blessed be He!' After that you must invoke the Angel San-dalfon by means of cabalistic formulae. Thereupon, he and his angel hosts will appear immediately.

"Be prepared with strong spices for the coming of these angels, so that they might revive you from the terror into which you will fall when you perceive the holy fire and the mighty whirlwind which will come in the wake of the Heavenly Host. Remember, when they appear you must fall upon your faces and recite the verse: 'Praised be His Name whose glorious kingdom is forever and ever!'

"After that the mighty Angel Sandalfon will reveal himself to you. You must then ask him what you should do in order to drive the spirit of evil from the world.

"If you do as I bid, and provided Almighty God wills it so, then you will be able to bring the Redemption for all the world."

After having blessed Rabbi Joseph and his disciples the Prophet Elijah vanished.

And Rabbi Joseph della Reyna and his five disciples did all that the Prophet Elijah had told them. When their fasting, vigils, prayers and austerities were over, a terrifying tumult arose in Heaven. The Angel Sandalfon with his host of seraphim swept down upon the earth amidst a whirlwind and with a pillar of flame before them. Seeing them, Rabbi Joseph and his disciples became faint with fear and fell upon their faces. But they smelled the strong spices and their energies returned.

Then they cried out: "Praised be His Name whose glorious kingdom is forever and ever!" Only then did they dare to look upon the angels clothed in flame and splendor.

The Angel Sandalfon now spoke and his voice sounded like the low muttering of thunder, "O sinful mortals! Where did you get the strength and the insolence to cause such a turmoil in all the Seven Heavens? How dare you trouble me and the Hosts of Heaven to descend to the sinful earth? I bid you desist from this madness!"

So great was the terror of Rabbi Joseph that he lost the power of speech. Finally he fortified his spirit and replied, "Holy Angel Sandalfon! Believe me, I have not done this for my glory but for the glory of the Creator, blessed be His Name, for the glory of the Holy Torah, for the glory of the grandchildren of Abraham, Isaac and Jacob! Forgive me my insolence, for I could not help myself.

"I could no longer look on the suffering of my people in Exile. I could no longer stand by watching our enemies trampling us underfoot in the dust. My only aim is to drive away the impure demons who defile the world, who dim the holy flame of our faith. I wish to return the *Shekhina* to the ancient luster it had when the Temple still stood in Jerusalem. Let God be my witness that my intention is pure and my course upright!

"Therefore, O Holy Angel, I beg you to help me! Show me the right path, teach me the right course, so that I can bring the Messiah, the Redeemer, down on earth!"

The Angel Sandalfon was filled with compassion as he looked upon Rabbi Joseph della Reyna.

"May God be with you until you reach your goal!" he cried. "Rest assured that all angels in Heaven are in agreement that the Messiah should come and bring the Redemption for the Jewish people who suffer in Exile. Yet I must warn you that you have undertaken a very difficult task, for Satan and the demons have untold power. Even we, the angels, cannot vanquish them. Only if God Himself stands by you will you be able to achieve your aim. But how can you expect God to support you unless He believes that the right time has come for the Messiah?"

"Again I must warn you: your path is full of folly. Should you fail you might make matters even worse, you might hand the victory to Satan and he will become more arrogant and do greater evil than hitherto to mankind."

Rabbi Joseph's heart overflowed with bitterness. Alas! Even the mighty Angel Sandalfon would not help him!

In the meantime, the five disciples lay prostrate upon the ground, their faces hidden in terror.

"Rise up—rise up!" cried Rabbi Joseph. "Unite with me in prayer! Perhaps all together we will be able to soften the hearts of the angels and they will agree to help us in our great work."

Once again Rabbi Joseph della Reyna pleaded with the Angel Sandalfon, "Help me, show me the right way!"

Sadly the Angel Sandalfon replied, "If I have come to you it is because you forced me by pronouncing the Ineffable Name, but alas, I cannot help you! I myself do not know the means by which you can triumph over Satan and the demons. My one duty is to guard the way along which the prayers of the righteous mount to Heaven and to bring them before the Throne of God. I have no power over Satan and do not know whether I can pit my strength against his.

"However, if you are so desperately determined to achieve your goal you must call upon the Angel Metatron and his hosts. They have been assigned by God to prevent Satan from growing stronger. Yet, I doubt very much whether you will be able to bring this great angel down to you. He resides in the Seventh Heaven right next to the Heavenly Throne. Therefore, not every prayer can penetrate up to him. Even should he hear you, I doubt whether you and your disciples will be able to survive the terror of his presence. Know that he appears as a pillar of fire and that his face is more dazzling than the sun. Therefore, I beg of you: abandon your plan, for it is madness!"

Still Rabbi Joseph would not submit.

"I know," said he brokenly, "that I am weak and insignificant. I know that it is impudence on my part to dare talk with angels and to contradict them. But I hope that the Ruler of the World, reading my heart, will not spurn my prayer and will aid me in the work that I have undertaken. O Angel of the World, help me! Tell me how I can bring the Angel Metatron down to earth."

"Since you insist," replied the Angel Sandalfon, "you and your disciples must do the following: You must fast forty more days and purify yourself twenty-one times each day in the Sea of Galilee. You must study Cabala and say your prayers incessantly. Both by day and by night must you purify your thoughts. You must eat still less than you have hitherto, and live on spices alone. After that you must recite the Ineffable Name formed by seventy-two letters and call upon Metatron, the Angel of this mystic name, to appear before you."

The Angel Sandalfon then gave Rabbi Joseph and his disciples his blessing, "May your spirits be strong and survive the terror of Metatron's presence!"

Then, followed by his hosts of Angels, he mounted to Heaven in a whirlwind.

The stubbornness of Rabbi Joseph della Reyna aroused all the angels in Heaven. Nothing was spoken of but his daring attempt to bring the Messiah down to earth. The Messiah himself was hopeful that soon he would have to descend on his white horse to the children of man.

Even his horse began to chafe and paw, eager to be let out of the Heavenly stable. Also, the Prophet Elijah took out his great *shofar* and began to practice on it, for he would be the one to announce the coming of the Messiah with a mighty blast.

When Satan got wind of the news he trembled at the danger that was threatening him. At the time when all the angels and seraphim in Heaven were rejoicing, he sat gnashing his teeth in the bottom-most regions of the lowest *Gehenna.* He then took counsel with his wife Lilith who upbraided him for doing nothing while their very existence was being threatened. Thereupon, Satan hurried off to press his complaints before God.

"The Angels are playing me a trick!" he cried. "They wish to make an end of me before my time has come! How, O Lord, can Messiah come when there are so many sinners among the Jews? As for this stubborn fool, Joseph della Reyna, give me permission to do with him what is just."

But God denied him his request, for the prayers that Rabbi Joseph and his disciples had intoned, their days and nights of fasting, their sacred reflection and austerities, stood around them like a fortified wall. Therefore, Satan had no power over them.

Yet Satan could not be silenced. God told him that, although his arguments were just, it still lay within God's power to hasten the Redemption even before the appointed day, if He but wished it. Moreover, if the Jews possessed such a saint as Rabbi Joseph della Reyna they were indeed worthy of the Messiah's quick coming.

"However," added God, "should Joseph della Reyna stray from righteousness by even the thickness of a hair, I will give you the power to bring his plan to naught!"

When Rabbi Joseph della Reyna told his disciples what the Angel Sandalfon had counselled him to do, they answered with one voice, "We will do whatever you require of us!"

They then left Tiberias and went up to a mountain fastness. They found a cave and made their home in it. Here they performed their austerities and vigils for forty days and forty nights, just as the Angel Sandalfon had said. Finally, they became released from all the tentacles of this sinful world and reached the highest degree of sanctity and virtue.

When the forty days were over they went farther into the wilderness and purified themselves in Lake Kishon. Then they recited the *Mincha* prayers with great fervor. After that they clasped hands and formed a mystic circle. They prayed that God might give them the necessary strength to survive the terror of the fiery presence of the Angel Metatron and of his angelic host.

Finally, Rabbi Joseph pronounced the Ineffable Name of God formed of seventy-two letters.

Thereupon, the earth become convulsed and trembled. Lightning and thunder rent the heavens and a whirlwind came.

Rabbi Joseph and his disciples stood firm, clasping hands in the mystic circle. They smelled strong spices to fortify their spirits and intoned prayers.

The Angel Metatron appeared, surrounded by his host of angels and seraphim.

"O sinful man!" cried the angels. "O puny creature of flesh and blood, wretched as a worm! How dare you storm the Heavens with your prayers and oblige the angels to come to earth?"

Rabbi Joseph and his students were filled with terror. Summoning up all his courage, Rabbi Joseph spoke at last.

"Holy angels, help me! Give me the strength to talk to you!"

The Angel Metatron then drew near and touched Rabbi Joseph, whereupon he lost all fear and spoke. "Believe me, I have no evil intention. All I want is to bring the Messiah in order to end the Exile of the Jewish people. Therefore, teach me how to vanquish Satan and his evil power."

The Angel Metatron became stern.

"Foolish man!" he cried. "All your efforts are in vain! Know that Satan is all powerful. He is fortified by a great wall of the sins of the Jewish people. How can you expect to break through where others have failed? Only when God wills that the Messiah should come will He come. Therefore, abandon your plan!"

But Rabbi Joseph was stubborn.

"Almighty God has helped me thus far and I've remained among the living," he said. "Therefore, I will not turn back!"

When the Angel Metatron saw that Rabbi Joseph could not be moved in his determination he was filled with compassion for him. He then advised him what to do.

He revealed to him all the mystic formulae, all the incantations and the Ineffable Name. With their aid, he said, Rabbi Joseph would succeed in capturing Satan and Lilith and thus drive all evil from the world. With that accomplished, the Messiah would surely come!

He also had him engrave on a metal plate the Ineffable Name and taught him how to use it. He warned him especially to guard himself against the weakness of pity towards evil after he had made captive Satan and Lilith. Under no circumstance was he to give them any food or any spices to smell. If he did, all his efforts would be wasted. He would thus only expose himself to the revenge of Satan.

When the Angel Metatron and his host had departed, Rabbi Joseph and his disciples began making preparations for their battle with the Evil One.

Rabbi Joseph della Reyna and his five disciples went up on Mount Sheir. On the way they met many wild dogs. These, they very well knew, were demons that Satan had sent in order to confuse and frighten them. But Rabbi Joseph pronounced an incantation and they vanished.

As they continued on their way they came to a snow-capped mountain that seemed to pierce the very Heavens. They then pronounced mystic formulae that the angels had taught them and the mountain vanished.

On the third day they came to a turbulent sea. Here too they recited mystic formulae and the ocean dried up before their very eyes.

Further on they found their way obstructed by an iron wall which reached to the sky. Behind it stood Satan, lying in wait for them. Rabbi Joseph took a knife on which was engraved one of the mystic names of God and with it he ripped the wall asunder.

They then ascended a towering mountain from the top of which they heard the loud barking of dogs. When they finally reached the summit Rabbi Joseph saw a hut. As he tried to enter, two frightfully big dogs sprang at his throat. Rabbi Joseph recognized them to be Satan and Lilith, so he quickly raised before them the metal plate with the Ineffable Name engraved upon it. Thereupon, they lost their evil power and slunk away.

The five disciples then bound the dogs with ropes on which were tied little metal amulets engraved with the mystic names of God. Immediately the dogs were transformed. They took on the appearance of humans except that they had wings and fiery eyes.

"Do give us something to eat," they whined.

But Rabbi Joseph recalled the Angel Metatron's warning against falling prey to the weakness of pity towards evil. So he gave them no food.

Rabbi Joseph and his disciples were now filled with indescribable bliss. At last, at last, they had succeeded in capturing Satan and Lilith! Now they would be able to bring Messiah down to earth!

"Let us hurry!" impatiently cried Rabbi Joseph della Reyna to his disciples. "We are already nearing our goal! Soon the Gates of Heaven will open wide for us and the Holy Messiah will come forth to welcome us!"

All this time Satan and Lilith were moaning in heartbreaking voices, "Help us! Give us something to eat! We're dying of hunger!"

Still Rabbi Joseph della Reyna hardened his heart against them.

When they saw that they could not swerve him Satan and Lilith asked wheedingly, "At least give us a smell of your spices or we perish!"

Now Rabbi Joseph was a compassionate man. He could not endure the sight of suffering in man or beast. Having triumphed over Satan and Lilith he thought he could now safely show a small measure of magnanimity towards them. He therefore gave them some of the strong spices to smell.

Immediately, tongues of searing flame shot from their nostrils. All their former strength returned to them. They tore away their bonds and summoned to their aid hosts of shrieking demons and devils.

Two of the disciples instantly died of terror. Two of them went out of their minds and wandered away. Only Rabbi Joseph and one disciple remained.

A terrible wailing was now heard in Heaven and the angels went into mourning. The Messiah wept and led his white horse back into its

Heavenly stall. Also the Prophet Elijah grieved and hid the great *shofar* of the Redemption. Then the voice of the Almighty sounded:

"Pay heed, O Joseph della Reyna! No human has the power to end the Exile! I alone, God, will hasten the Redemption of the Jewish people when the right time comes!"

Explanatory Notes

Glossary of Hebrew terms:

Cabala: medieval mystical theology.

Gematriot: a system of using the numerical value of letters to connect words and phrases.

Gehenna: Hell.

Mincha: the daily afternoon service.

Shekhina: the aspect of the Godhead which accompanies the Jews in exile; therefore that aspect of God which is immanent rather than transcendent.

Shofar: ram's horn.

Talith: prayer shawl.

Tefillin: prayer phylacteries.

Zohar: the basic book of the Cabala. Though attributed to Shimeon ben Yohai, a Talmudic figure (see Unit VII), it was actually composed in medieval Spain.

Questions for Discussion

Do you think Joseph della Reyna should have tried to force the coming of the Messiah?

If not, why do you think none of the angels, etc., stopped him by withholding their aid?

In the end, did he make things worse?

Do you think he was wrong to have "a weakness of pity towards evil"?

Should the bringing of the Messiah come about through cruelty, even to Satan? Or is it naive to think that the Messiah could come without some pain? Is some cruelty a necessary price to pay for bringing about a greater good?

Why does the story end by God stating that He alone will bring the Messiah? In effect, do you agree with God or Joseph della Reyna?

What does the story tell us about trying to accomplish good in a world full of evil?

What did Joseph della Reyna have to sacrifice even on the way to his goal? What was he not willing to sacrifice at the end? What does this tell us about the price to be paid for doing good?

How would you have acted in Joseph della Reyna's situation or in an analagous one?

Suggested Questions for Children

Was Joseph della Reyna right to take pity on Satan, or was it a foolish thing to do?

We close our Shabbat study with the concluding prayer on page 40.

UNIT X

the struggle to preserve tradition in a changing world

This selection raises the issues involved in keeping a spiritual tradition alive and meaningful in a changing secular world. The parable, attributed to Rabbi Yehoshua Lovaine, a fictional rabbi, was written first in Hebrew and Yiddish and then in English, by Rabbi Tsvi Blanchard.

Rabbi Blanchard, who holds a Ph.D. in Philosophy and an M.S. in Clinical Psychology, has been teaching Jewish Studies at Washington University in St. Louis for ten years and now is the Director of Mosad-Or, a traditional institute for the study of Jewish texts.

The Sheep of the Hidden Valley[20]

By Tsvi Blanchard

There was once a tailor in a valley so small, and so far away, that you have probably never heard of it. The tailor was a man of great skill. His excellent material, perfect stitching and precision in fitting assured that his customers were always satisfied. When the clothes became torn, the tailor could mend them so that they were almost like new. Despite his great skill, the tailor was a troubled man. Even when he used the best of materials his clothes did not last forever. They sometimes lasted out the life of a customer, but rarely was a suit passed down from father to son.

One night the tailor dreamt that he was wandering about the surrounding towns. Suddenly he found a valley hidden away from the eyes of the world. In this valley were sheep with thick coats of beautiful wool. In his

102

dream, he spoke to a man who confided to him the many intricate details of raising sheep whose wool was fine as golden thread, soft as baby's skin, as shining as a star, and as firm when woven as the resolve of a wise man. The tailor awoke from his dream determined to seek out the valley and its sheep. For many years he travelled the countryside without success.

At last behind a waterfall at which he had stopped to refresh himself, the tailor found a hidden valley in which grazed sheep with marvelous wool. In the real valley, unlike the one of his dream, there was no shepherd to guide him in raising the sheep. In moments of deep concentration, the tailor was able to remember the special rules communicated to him in his dream. He dedicated himself to raising these sheep, and followed the rules for their care scrupulously.

Wishing to share his discovery with the villagers, his beloved friends, the tailor announced that he would sew new clothes for all adults in the village. He sheared his sheep, wove their wool into cloth, and began to sew the new garments. The tailor found to his surprise that he had just enough cloth to make clothes for every man and woman in his village. Although the tailor guarded them well, the sheep somehow disappeared within a week of their shearing, and no more clothing could be sewn from their splendid wool.

The new garments were a delight to the village. The people discovered that this clothing, so warm and snug in winter, was never uncomfortable even in the hottest heat of summer. The rain did not ruin these fine clothes nor did the years wear them thin. When they were torn through carelessness, it needed but a stitch to restore them. These were charmed garments, and the villagers of that generation counted themselves blessed.

A boy reaching the age of manhood approached his father in secret. He asked his father to acquire for him a fine suit of clothes like the ones owned by the adults in the village. He too would soon be a full member of his village, and, he argued, he should have as splendid a garment as any one else. When the father explained that there were no more miraculous garments, the boy cried bitterly. Finally the father, out of his great love for the boy, took off his own coat and gave it to his son. A great miracle followed. Having put on his father's coat over his own garments, the boy found that his clothing was transformed into the material of his father's garments. Soon it was discovered that whenever a child near the age of adulthood put on his parent's cloak, the child's own clothing turned to the cloth woven from the marvelous wool of the sheep of the hidden valley.

As the young people grew, they found the clothes changing to fit them.

Arms lengthened, chests filled out, and at the same time the garments had longer sleeves and fuller breadth. However a person changed, if he became fatter or thinner, wider or narrower, straighter or more bent with age, the miraculous clothing fit exactly.

The village became famous throughout the area and many envied the fine garments. People in the surrounding towns began to gossip, and they whispered that wearing the same clothes continually showed the backwardness of the villagers. They said that it made the villagers boring. Believing the garments worn by the young to be those of their parents, they bitingly asked: who wears the clothes of dead people? They did not know the secret of the garments or their source, so they did not understand.

After many years, some say generations, the trust of the village itself was undermined and many came to doubt what their own eyes had seen. The village became divided. Some sold or gave away their old garments, preferring to wear the stylish new clothing they found in the surrounding towns. These who bought new clothes found that they soon wore out. When they tore they could not be restored and had to be discarded. Their ancestral garments, when worn by others, lost their special properties. The garments, once the pride of the town, became rags for the poor in the neighboring towns.

Others in the village tried refashioning the old garments. They dyed the new colors, lengthened and shortened hems, and restitched the seams to fit the newer fashions. Their newly restyled clothes did not wear well and, as with the others, were discarded. Still others in the village desperately tried to prevent the slightest change in the clothing. They refused to allow the alteration of the garments, even a stitch. But their clothes grew stiff about them, losing their ability to fit throughout the whole of a person's life. Finally, these garments too were discarded.

Fewer and fewer of the original coats were to be found. As the years passed many in the village began to doubt that there ever were such marvelous clothes. They could not believe in the funny story about the tailor, his dream and his hidden valley. Where was this valley? What proof was there that such a tailor had ever existed? Who trusts dreams? And most of all, where were these so-called magic garments?

The few who claimed to own original coats were regarded as half-crazy or deluded, or at the least as very poorly dressed. Among those who still wore the old coats there was a desire, born from the love of their neighbors, to restore the miracle of their special clothing. They alone knew the value of the clothing. They alone knew how much superior were the original garments to the new ones. There arose among them a question: will we, they asked, need once again a tailor who dreams of wondrous sheep, and can then find them? Or, they wondered, do we simply need to collect the worn rags and reweave them into the fine garments? They have not yet answered this question.

Questions for Discussion

Why was the tailor troubled that the clothes he made himself did not last forever? Should he have been?

Why did it take many years to find the hidden valley? Where was it?

Why didn't the tailor show the hidden valley to the other people of the village?

What happened to the clothes? How did children acquire them? What does all this signify?

How did other people criticize the villagers and their clothes?

Why do you think the villagers' ancestral clothes lost their special properties when sold to other people?

What happened to those who tried to style the ancestral garments? To those who tried not to alter them in any way? Why?

What is the meaning of the final question? What do you think is the answer?

Suggested Questions for Children

Why do you think the villagers came to doubt the specialness of their clothes? Do you ever take things for granted?

Can the scorn or laughter of others make you doubt something you know is true?

Is something old always bad or at least old-fashioned?

Don't old things have to be discarded if there is to be progress, even if this is a painful process?

Isn't it part of growing up to put aside toys, etc., that are old or babyish?

Would you have believed in the hidden valley? Most strange things are dismissed as fantasy; but what if one unusual thing is true? How would you know whether to believe it or not?

We close our Shabbat study with the concluding prayer on page 40.

UNIT XI

BEING JEWISH IN THE MODERN WORLD

The ambivalence many Jews feel about retaining their Jewish identity in the modern world is the theme of the short story *The Jewbird,* by Bernard Malamud. Malamud is a leading American Jewish novelist, known for such works as *The Assistant, The Magic Barrel, Idiots First,* and *Dubin's Lives.* His book *The Fixer,* a fictionalized account of the Beilis trial, won a National Book Award and the Pulitzer Prize (1967).

The Jewbird[21]

By Bernard Malamud

The window was open so the skinny bird flew in. Flappity-flap with its frazzled black wings. That's how it goes. It's open, you're in. Closed, you're out and that's your fate. The bird wearily flapped through the open kitchen window of Harry Cohen's top-floor apartment on First Avenue near the lower East River. On a rod on the wall hung an escaped canary cage, its door wide open, but this black-type longbeaked bird—its ruffled head and small dull eyes, crossed a little, making it look like a dissipated crow—landed if not smack on Cohen's thick lamb chop, at least on the table, close by. The frozen foods salesman was sitting at supper with his wife and young son on a hot August evening a year ago. Cohen, a heavy man with hairy chest and beefy shorts; Edie, in skinny yellow shorts and red halter; and their ten-year-old Morris (after her father)—Maurie, they called him, a nice kid though not overly bright—were all in the city after two weeks out, because Cohen's mother was dying. They had been enjoying Kingston, New York, but drove back when Mama got sick in her flat in the Bronx.

"Right on the table," said Cohen, putting down his beer glass and swatting at the bird. "Son of a bitch."

"Harry, take care with your language," Edie said, looking at Maurie, who watched every move.

The bird cawed hoarsely and with a flap of its bedraggled wings—feathers tufted this way and that—rose heavily to the top of the open kitchen door, where it perched staring down.

"Gevalt, a pogrom!"

"It's a talking bird," said Edie in astonishment.

"In Jewish," said Maurie.

"Wise guy," muttered Cohen. He gnawed on his chop, then put down the bone. "So if you can talk, say what's your business. What do you want here?"

"If you can't spare a lamb chop," said the bird, "I'll settle for a piece of herring with a crust of bread. You can't live on your nerve forever."

"This ain't a restaurant," Cohen replied. "All I'm asking is what brings you to this address?"

"The window was open," the bird sighed; adding after a moment, "I'm running. I'm flying but I'm also running."

"From whom?" asked Edie with interest.

"Anti-Semeets."

"Anti-Semites?" they all said.

"That's from who."

"What kind of anti-Semites bother a bird?" Edie asked.

"Any kind," said the bird, "also including eagles, vultures, and hawks. And once in a while some crows will take your eyes out."

"But aren't you a crow?"

"Me? I'm a Jewbird."

Cohen laughed heartily. "What do you mean by that?"

The bird began dovening. He prayed without Book or tallith, but with passion. Edie bowed her head though not Cohen. And Maurie rocked back and forth with the prayer, looking up with one wide-open eye.

When the prayer was done Cohen remarked, "No hat, no phylacteries?"

"I'm an old radical."

"You're sure you're not some kind of a ghost or dybbuk?"

"Not a dybbuk," answered the bird, "though one of my relatives had such an experience once. It's all over now, thanks God. They freed her from a former lover, a crazy jealous man. She's now the mother of two wonderful children."

"Birds?" Cohen asked slyly.

"Why not?"

"What kind of birds?"

"Like me. Jewbirds."

Cohen tipped back in his chair and guffawed. "That's a big laugh. I've heard of a Jewfish but not a Jewbird."

"We're once removed." The bird rested on one skinny leg, then on the other. "Please, could you spare maybe a piece of herring with a small crust of bread?"

Edie got up from the table.

"What are you doing?" Cohen asked her.

"I'll clear the dishes."

Cohen turned to the bird. "So what's your name, if you don't mind saying?"

"Call me Schwartz."

"He might be an old Jew changed into a bird by somebody," said Edie, removing a plate.

"Are you?" asked Harry, lighting a cigar.

"Who knows?" answered Schwartz, "Does God tell us everything?"

Maurie got up on his chair. "What kind of herring?" he asked the bird in excitement.

"Get down, Maurie, or you'll fall," ordered Cohen.

"If you haven't got matjes, I'll take schmaltz," said Schwartz.

"All we have is marinated, with slices of onion—in a jar," said Edie.

"If you'll open for me the jar I'll eat marinated. Do you have also, if you don't mind, a piece of rye bread—the spitz?"

Edie thought she had.

"Feed him out on the balcony," Cohen said. He spoke to the bird. "After that take off."

Schwartz closed both bird eyes. "I'm tired and it's a long way."

"Which direction are you headed, north or south?"

Schwartz, barely lifting his wings, shrugged.

"You don't know where you're going?"

"Where there's charity I'll go."

"Let him stay, papa," said Maurie. "He's only a bird."

"So stay the night," Cohen said, "but no longer."

In the morning Cohen ordered the bird out of the house but Maurie cried, so Schwartz stayed for a while. Maurie was still on vacation from school and his friends were away. He was lonely and Edie enjoyed the fun he had, playing with the bird.

"He's no trouble at all," she told Cohen, "and besides his appetite is very small."

"What'll you do when he makes dirty?"

"He flies across the street in a tree when he makes dirty, and if nobody passes below, who notices?"

"So all right," said Cohen, "but I'm dead set against it. I warn you he ain't gonna stay here long."

"What have you got against the poor bird?"

"Poor bird, my ass. He's a foxy bastard. He thinks he's a Jew."

"What difference does it make what he thinks?"

"A Jewbird, what a chuzpah. One false move and he's out on his drumsticks."

At Cohen's insistence Schwartz lived out on the balcony in a new wooden birdhouse Edie had bought him.

"With many thanks," said Schwartz, "though I would rather have a human roof over my head. You know how it is at my age. I like the warm, the windows, the smell of cooking. I would also be glad to see once in a while the *Jewish Morning Journal* and have now and then a schnapps because it helps my breathing, thanks God. But whatever you give me, you won't hear complaints."

However, when Cohen brought home a bird feeder full of dried corn, Schwartz said, "Impossible."

Cohen was annoyed. "What's the matter, crosseyes, is your life getting too good for you? Are you forgetting what it means to be migratory? I'll bet a helluva lot of crows you happen to be acquainted with, Jews or otherwise, would give their eyeteeth to eat this corn."

Schwartz did not answer. What can you say to a grubber yung?

"Not for my digestion," he later explained to Edie. "Cramps. Herring is better even if it makes you thirsty. At least rainwater don't cost anything." He laughed sadly in breathy caws.

And herring, thanks to Edie, who knew where to shop, was what Schwartz got, with an occasional piece of potato pancake, and even a bit of soupmeat when Cohen wasn't looking.

When school began in September, before Cohen would once again suggest giving the bird the boot, Edie prevailed on him to wait a little while until Maurie adjusted.

"To deprive him right now might hurt his school work, and you know what trouble we had last year."

"So okay, but sooner or later the bird goes. That I promise you."

Schwartz, though nobody had asked him, took on full responsibility for Maurie's performance in school. In return for favors granted, when he was let in for an hour or two at night, he spent most of his time overseeing the boy's lessons. He sat on top of the dresser near Maurie's desk as he laboriously wrote out his homework. Maurie was a restless type and Schwartz gently kept him to his studies. He also listened to him practice his screechy violin, taking a few minutes off now and then to rest his ears in the bathroom. And they afterwards played dominoes. The boy was an indifferent checker player and it was impossible to teach him chess. When he was sick, Schwartz read him comic books though he personally disliked them. But Maurie's work improved in school and even his violin teacher admitted his playing was better. Edie gave Schwartz credit for these improvements though the bird pooh-poohed them.

Yet he was proud there was nothing lower than C minuses on Maurie's report card, and on Edie's insistence celebrated with a little schnapps.

"If he keeps up like this," Cohen said, "I'll get him in an Ivy League college for sure."

"Oh I hope so," sighed Edie.

But Schwartz shook his head. "He's a good boy—you don't have to worry. He won't be a shicker or a wifebeater, God forbid, but a scholar he'll never be, if you know what I mean, although maybe a good mechanic. It's no disgrace in these times."

"If I were you," Cohen said, angered, "I'd keep my big snoot out of other people's private business."

"Harry, please," said Edie.

"My goddamn patience is wearing out. That crosseyes butts into everything."

Though he wasn't exactly a welcome guest in the house, Schwartz gained a few ounces although he did not improve in appearance. He looked bedraggled as ever, his feathers unkempt, as though he had just flown out of a snowstorm. He spent, he admitted, little time taking care of himself. Too much to think about. "Also outside plumbing," he told Edie. Still there was more glow to his eyes so that though Cohen went on calling him crosseyes he said it less emphatically.

Liking his situation, Schwartz tried tactfully to stay out of Cohen's way, but one night when Edie was at the movies and Maurie was taking a hot shower, the frozen foods salesman began a quarrel with the bird.

"For Christ sake, why don't you wash yourself sometimes? Why must you always stink like a dead fish?"

"Mr. Cohen, if you'll pardon me, if somebody eats garlic he will smell from garlic. I eat herring three times a day. Feed me flowers and I will smell like flowers."

"Who's obligated to feed you anything at all? You're lucky to get herring."

"Excuse me, I'm not complaining," said the bird. "You're complaining."

"What's more," said Cohen, "even from out on the balcony I can hear you snoring away like a pig. It keeps me awake at night."

"Snoring," said Schwartz, "isn't a crime, thanks God."

"All in all you are a goddamn pest and free loader. Next thing you'll want to sleep in bed next to my wife."

"Mr. Cohen," said Schwartz, "on this rest assured. A bird is a bird."

"So you say, but how do I know you're a bird and not some kind of a goddamn devil?"

"If I was a devil you would know already. And I don't mean because your son's good marks."

"Shut up, you bastard bird," shouted Cohen.

"Grubber yung," cawed Schwartz, rising to the tips of his talons, his long wings outstretched.

Cohen was about to lunge for the bird's scrawny neck but Maurie came out of the bathroom, and for the rest of the evening until Schwartz's bedtime on the balcony, there was pretended peace.

But the quarrel had deeply disturbed Schwartz and he slept badly. His snoring woke him, and awake, he was fearful of what would become of him. Wanting to stay out of Cohen's way, he kept to the birdhouse as much as possible. Cramped by it, he paced back and forth on the balcony ledge, or sat on the birdhouse roof, staring into space. In the evening, while overseeing Maurie's lessons, he often fell asleep. Awakening, he nervously hopped around exploring the four corners of the room. He spent much time in Maurie's closet, and carefully examined his bureau drawers when they were left open. And once when he found a large paper bag on the floor, Schwartz poked his way into it to investigate what possibilities were. The boy was amused to see the bird in the paper bag.

"He wants to build a nest," he said to his mother.

Edie, sensing Schwartz's unhappiness, spoke to him quietly.

"Maybe if you did some of the things my husband wants you, you would get along better with him."

"Give me a for instance," Schwartz said.

"Like take a bath, for instance."

"I'm too old for baths," said the bird. "My feathers fall out without baths."

"He says you have a bad smell."

"Everybody smells. Some people smell because of their thoughts or because who they are. My bad smell comes from the food I eat. What does his come from?"

"I better not ask him or it might make him mad," said Edie.

In late November Schwartz froze on the balcony in the fog and cold, and especially on rainy days he woke with stiff joints and could barely move his wings. Already he felt twinges of rheumatism. He would have liked to spend more time in the warm house, particularly when Maurie was in school and Cohen at work. But though Edie was goodhearted and might have sneaked him in in the morning, just to thaw out, he was afraid to ask her. In the meantime Cohen, who had been reading articles about the migration of birds, came out on the balcony one night after work when Edie was in the kitchen preparing pot roast, and peeking into the bird-house, warned Schwartz to be on his way soon if he knew what was good for him. "Time to hit the flyways."

"Mr. Cohen, why do you hate me so much?" asked the bird. "What did I do to you?"

"Because you're an A-number-one trouble maker, that's why. What's more, whoever heard of a Jewbird? Now scat or it's open war."

But Schwartz stubbornly refused to depart so Cohen embarked on a campaign of harrassing him, meanwhile hiding it from Edie and Maurie. Maurie hated violence and Cohen didn't want to leave a bad impression. He thought maybe if he played dirty tricks on the bird he would fly off without being physically kicked out. The vacation was over, let him make his easy living off the fat of somebody else's land. Cohen worried about the effect of the bird's departure on Maurie's schooling but decided to take the chance, first, because the boy now seemed to have the knack of studying— give the black bird-bastard credit—and second, because Schwartz was driving him bats by being there always, even in his dreams.

The frozen foods salesman began his campaign against the bird by mixing watery cat food with the herring slices in Schwartz's dish. He also blew

up and popped numerous paper bags outside the birdhouse as the bird
slept, and when he had got Schwartz good and nervous, though not enough
to leave, he brought a full-grown cat into the house, supposedly a gift for
little Maurie, who had always wanted a pussy. The cat never stopped
springing up at Schwartz whenever he saw him, one day managing to claw
out several of his tailfeathers. And even at lesson time, when the cat was
usually excluded from Maurie's room, though somehow or other he quickly
found his way in at the end of the lesson, Schwartz was desperately fearful
of his life and flew from pinnacle to pinnacle—light fixture to clothes-tree
to door-top—in order to elude the beast's wet jaws.

Once when the bird complained to Edie how hazardous his existence
was, she said, "Be patient, Mr. Schwartz. When the cat gets to know you
better he won't try to catch you any more."

"When he stops trying we will both be in Paradise," Schwartz
answered. "Do me a favor and get rid of him. He makes my whole life
worry. I'm losing feathers like a tree loses leaves."

"I'm awfully sorry but Maurie likes the pussy and sleeps with it."

What could Schwartz do? He worried but came to no decision, being
afraid to leave. So he ate the herring garnished with cat food, tried hard not
to hear the paper bags bursting like fire crackers outside the birdhouse at
night, and lived terror-stricken closer to the ceiling than the floor, as the
cat, his tail flicking, endlessly watched him.

Weeks went by. Then on the day after Cohen's mother had died in her
flat in the Bronx, when Maurie came home with a zero on an arithmetic
test, Cohen, enraged, waited until Edie had taken the boy to his violin
lesson, then openly attacked the bird. He chased him with a broom on the
balcony and Schwartz frantically flew back and forth, finally escaping into
his birdhouse. Cohen triumphantly reached in, and grabbing both skinny
legs, dragged the bird out, cawing loudly, his wings wildly beating. He
whirled the bird around and around his head. But Schwartz, as he moved in
circles, managed to swoop down and catch Cohen's nose in his beak, and
hung on for dear life. Cohen cried out in great pain, punched the bird with
his fist, and tugging at its legs with all his might, pulled his nose free. Again
he swung the yawking Schwartz around until the bird grew dizzy, then
with a furious heave, flung him into the night. Schwartz sank like stone into
the street. Cohen then tossed the birdhouse and feeder after him, listening
at the ledge until they crashed on the sidewalk below. For a full hour,
broom in hand, his heart palpitating and nose throbbing with pain, Cohen

waited for Schwartz to return but the broken-hearted bird didn't.

That's the end of that dirty bastard, the salesman thought and went in. Edie and Maurie had come home.

"Look," said Cohen, pointing to his bloody nose swollen three times its normal size, "what that sonofabitchy bird did. It's a permanent scar."

"Where is he now?" Edie asked, frightened.

"I threw him out and he flew away. Good riddance."

Nobody said no, though Edie touched a handkerchief to her eyes and Maurie rapidly tried the nine times table and found he knew approximately half.

In the spring when the winter's snow had melted, the boy, moved by a memory, wandered in the neighborhood, looking for Schwartz. He found a dead black bird in a small lot near the river, his two wings broken, neck twisted, and both bird-eyes plucked clean.

"Who did it to you, Mr. Schwartz?" Maurie wept.

"Anti-Semeets," Edie said later.

Questions for Discussion

Who is Schwartz the Jewbird?

What kind of relationship do Edie and Maurie have with Schwartz? Does it change during the story?

What relationship does Cohen have with Schwartz? Why? What does Cohen want from Schwartz? Is he ever "nice" to Schwartz?

Does Cohen hate Schwartz? If so, why?

Is Cohen afraid of Schwartz? If so, why?

Why are only Schwartz and Cohen referred to by their last names?

What is the significance of what Schwartz does about Maurie's studies?

Who are the anti-Semites?

What does the end of the story mean?

Suggested Questions for Children

Why does Cohen treat Schwartz the way he does?

Who is Schwartz?

Are you ever embarrassed by the appearance or deeds of other Jews? Are you ever embarrassed about being Jewish yourself?

We close our Shabbat study with the concluding prayer on page 40.

114

isRael and the diaspora

The relationship of the Diaspora to Israel is dealt with in *The Fable of the Goat* by S.Y. Agnon. Agnon (1888–1970) was born in Poland, but settled in Israel at the age of 20. He won the Nobel Prize for Literature in 1966, and his stories and novels have become classics of Hebrew literature. While drawing upon traditional sayings and motifs, they deal with contemporary spiritual concerns.

The Fable of the Goat appears on the surface to be a charming child's story, and in fact it is to be found in many collections of tales for children. On another level, however, it grapples with questions that may not be very comprehensible to a child. It presents many complex themes. We encounter a reflection of the traditional healing qualities of Israel, symbolized by the goat's milk, as well as the human frailties and the lack of faith which stand in the way of redemption and return to the Holy Land. The fragility of a dream fulfilled and the difficulties of sustaining the mystic faith in miracles in the Diaspora are apparent in the behavior of both the father "groaning from his heart" and the son who achieves the peace of living in the land of Israel. Indeed, the ideal of life in Israel would seem to be a distillation of the Diaspora experience. As one critic, Arnold Band, has written:

> In less than three pages Agnon has concentrated here many of the motifs treated at greater length in other works: the hero sick with a strange illness and the concomitant problem of finding the proper cure; the difference between the generations, reversed here since the writer wanted to emphasize the contrast between the son's innocence and the father's experience; the realm of sanctity embodied by Eretz Yisrael and the Sabbath; the hero's alienation from the realm of sanctity because of his own deeds.[22]

In this short tale, then, Agnon contrasts an Israel, a paradise full of youth, innocence and spirituality, with a Diaspora symbolized by an old, sick man. This vision is a challenge to Jews living in the Diaspora and calls for a response from each of us.

The Fable of the Goat[23]

By S.Y. Agnon

The tale is told of an old man who groaned from his heart. The doctors were sent for, and they advised him to drink goat's milk. He went out and bought a she-goat and brought her into his home. Not many days passed before the goat disappeared. They went out to search for her but did not find her. She was not in the yard and not in the garden, not on the roof of the House of Study and not by the spring, not in the hills and not in the fields. She tarried several days and then returned by herself; and when she returned, her udder was full of a great deal of milk, the taste of which was as the taste of Eden. Not just once, but many times she disappeared from the house. They would go out in search for her and would not find her until she returned by herself with her udder full of milk that was sweeter than honey and whose taste was the taste of Eden.

One time the old man said to his son, "My son, I desire to know where she goes and whence she brings this milk which is sweet to my palate and a balm to all my bones."

His son said to him, "Father, I have a plan."

He said to him, "What is it?"

The son got up and brought a length of cord. He tied it to the goat's tail. His father said to him, "What are you doing, my son?"

He said to him, "I am tying a cord to the goat's tail, so that when I feel a pull on it I will know that she has decided to leave and I can catch the end of the cord and follow her on her way."

The old man nodded his head and said to him, "My son, if your heart is wise, my heart too will rejoice."

The youth tied the cord to the goat's tail and minded it carefully. When the goat set off, he held the cord in his hand and did not let it slacken until the goat was well on her way and he was following her. He was dragged along behind her until he came to a cave. The goat went into the cave, and the youth followed her, holding the cord. They walked thus for an hour or two, or maybe even a day or two. The goat wagged her tail and bleated, and the cave came to an end.

When they emerged from the cave, the youth saw lofty mountains, and hills full of the choicest fruit, and a fountain of living waters that flowed down from the mountains; and the wind wafted all manner of perfumes. The goat climbed up a tree by clutching at the ribbed leaves. Carob fruits

116

full of honey dropped from the tree, and she ate of the carobs and drank of the garden's fountain.

The youth stood and called to the wayfarers: "I adjure you, good people, tell me where I am, and what is the name of this place?"

They answered him, "You are in the Land of Israel, and you are close by Safed."

The youth lifted up his eyes to the heavens and said, "Blessed be the Omnipresent, blessed be He who has brought me to the Land of Israel." He kissed the soil and sat down under the tree.

He said, "Until the day breathe and the shadows flee away, I shall sit on the hill under this tree. Then I shall go home and bring my father and mother to the Land of Israel." As he was sitting thus and feasting his eyes on the holiness of the Land of Israel, he heard a voice proclaiming:

"Come, let us go out to greet the Sabbath Queen."

And he saw men like angels, wrapped in white shawls, with boughs of myrtle in their hands, and all the houses were lit with a great many candles. He perceived that the eve of Sabbath would arrive with the darkening, and that he would not be able to return. He uprooted a reed and dipped it in gallnuts, from which the ink for the writing of Torah scrolls is made. He took a piece of paper and wrote a letter to his father:

"From the ends of the earth I lift up my voice in song to tell you that I have come in peace to the Land of Israel. Here I sit, close by Safed, the holy city, and I imbibe its sanctity. Do not inquire how I arrived here but hold onto this cord which is tied to the goat's tail and follow the footsteps of the goat; then your journey will be secure, and you will enter the Land of Israel."

The youth rolled up the note and placed it in the goat's ear. He said to himself: When she arrives at Father's house, Father will pat her on the head, and she will flick her ears. The note will fall out, Father will pick it up and read what is written on it. Then he will take up the cord and follow the goat to the Land of Israel.

The goat returned to the old man, but she did not flick her ears, and the note did not fall. When the old man saw that the goat had returned without his son, he clapped his hands to his head and began to cry and weep and wail, "My son, my son, where are you? My son, would that I might die in your stead, my son, my son!"

So he went, weeping and mourning over his son, for he said, "An evil beast has devoured him, my son is assuredly rent in pieces!"

And he refused to be comforted, saying, "I will go down to my grave in mourning for my son."

And whenever he saw the goat, he would say, "Woe to the father who banished his son, and woe to her who drove him from the world!"

The old man's mind would not be at peace until he sent for the butcher to slaughter the goat. The butcher came and slaughtered the goat. As they were skinning her, the note fell out of her ear. The old man picked up the note and said, "My son's handwriting!"

When he had read all that his son had written, he clapped his hands to his head and cried, "*Vay! Vay!* Woe to the man who robs himself of his own good fortune, and woe to the man who requites good with evil!"

He mourned over the goat many days and refused to be comforted, saying, "Woe to me, for I could have gone up to the Land of Israel in one bound, and now I must suffer out my days in this exile!"

Since that time the mouth of the cave has been hidden from the eye, and there is no longer a short way. And that youth, if he has not died, shall bear fruit in his old age, full of sap and richness, calm and peaceful in the Land of the Living.

Questions for Discussion

What is the symbolism of:

> the old man who groaned from his heart
> the goat and her milk
> the son
> the cord
> what the son saw in Israel
> the message?

Why didn't the son himself return through the cave?

Why did the father kill the goat which nourished him?

Was following the goat the only way the son could have gone to Israel? The only way for the father?

Why is the mouth of the cave hidden away?

Why do you think it was the son and not the father who went to Israel?

What is the story saying about Israel and the Diaspora? Do you agree?

We close our Shabbat study with the concluding prayer on page 40.

footnotes

1. Erich Fromm, *You Shall Be As Gods* (New York: Holt, Rinehart and Winston, 1966), p. 197.
2. Abraham Joshua Heschel, *The Sabbath* (New York: Noonday Press, 1975), p. 28.
3. Ahad Ha'am, *Al Parashat Derakim*, Vol. III, p. 30. Quoted in: Abraham E. Millgram, *Sabbath, the Day of Delight* (Philadelphia: Jewish Publication Society, 1949), p. 253.
4. Samuel Dresner, *The Jew in American Life* (New York: Crown Publishers, 1963), p. 146.
5. "Prayer of a Jewish Woman," translated from the Yiddish by Arthur Green. In: Richard Siegel, Michael Strassfeld, Sharon Strassfeld, eds., *The First Jewish Catalog* (Philadelphia: Jewish Publication Society, 1973), p. 42.
6. Eliezer Berkovits, *God, Man and History* (New York: Jonathan David Publishers), p. 123.
7. Isaac Leib Peretz, "The Treasure." In: Millgram, *op. cit.*, pp. 261–265.
8. *Mimekor Yisrael*, Vol. I (Bloomington, Indiana: Indiana University Press; Philadelphia: Jewish Publication Society, 1976), pp. 24–26.
9. *Pirkei Avot*, 2:13–19.
10. *Babylonian Talmud*, Baba Metzia 59b.
11. *Ibid.*, Sanhedrin 68a.
12. Genesis 26:34–28:9.
13. Michael Strassfeld, *Rebecca's Last Words.* In: *Jewish Calendar* (New York: Universe, 1978).
14. Moses Maimonides, *Mishneh Torah*, section "Mattanot le'aniyim" ("Gifts to the Poor"), 7:3, 5–7, 9–10, 13; 9:1, 15–16; 10:5, 7–14.
15. Hugh Nissenson, "Charity." From: *In the Reign of Peace* (New York: Farrar, Straus & Giroux, 1970), pp. 51–63.
16. Abraham Joshua Heschel, *The Sabbath* (New York: Farrar, Straus & Giroux, 1975), pp. 35–37. Based on *Babylonian Talmud*, Shabbat 33b; *Maaseh Book*.
17. Heschel, *op. cit.*, pp. 41, 47–48.
18. Irving Rosenbaum, ed., *Holocaust and Halakhah* (New York: Ktav Publishing, 1976), pp. 25–27. The Library of Jewish Law and Ethics Series.
19. Nathan Ausubel, ed., *A Treasury of Jewish Folklore* (New York: Crown Publishers, 1948), pp. 206–215.
20. Tsvi Blanchard, "The Sheep of the Hidden Valley," translated from the Yid-

dish and Hebrew by the author. In: Howard Schwartz, ed., *Imperial Messages* (New York: Avon Books, 1976), pp. 271–273.

21. Bernard Malamud, "The Jewbird." From: *Idiots First* (New York: Farrar, Straus & Giroux, 1963), pp. 101–113.

22. Arnold Band, *From Nostalgia to Nightmare: A Study in the Fiction of S.Y. Agnon* (Los Angeles: University of California Press, 1968).

23. S.Y. Agnon, "The Fable of the Goat," translated from the Hebrew by Barney Rubin. From: *Twenty-one Stories* (New York: Schocken Books, 1970), pp. 26–29.

BIBLIOGRAPhY

Section I of this bibliography lists sources of further *knowledge about Shabbat*; Section II names books containing further *texts for reading on Shabbat*. Still more texts may be found via the bibliographies in some of the books named in Section II.

I. About Shabbat

Central Conference of Reform Rabbis. *A Shabbat Manual* (New York: Ktav, 1972).

Dresner, Samuel. *The Sabbath* (New York: The Burning Bush Press, 1970).

Grunfeld, Dayan I. *The Sabbath: A Guide to Its Understanding and Observance* (New York: Feldheim, 1959).

Heschel, Abraham Joshua. *The Sabbath: Its Meaning for Modern Man* (New York: The Noonday Press, 1975).

Siegel, Richard, Strassfeld, Michael, and Strassfeld, Sharon, eds. *The Jewish Catalog* (Philadelphia: Jewish Publication Society, 1973).

II. Texts for Shabbat

Bible

Chavel, Charles. *Ramban Commentary on the Torah* (New York: Shilo Publishing House, 1971). Translation of a classical medieval commentary.

Ginzberg, Louis. *Legends of the Bible* (Philadelphia: Jewish Publication Society, 1956).

Leibowitz, Nehama. *Studies in Bereshit (Genesis)* (New York: World Zionist Organization, 1974). One in a series on various books of the Bible.

Plaut, Gunther. *The Torah: A Modern Commentary*, Volume 1: Genesis (New York: Union of American Hebrew Congregations, 1976). Subsequent volumes on other books of the Bible.

Rosenbaum, M., and Silberman, A. *Pentateuch with Rashi Commentary* (New York: Hebrew Publishing Co., 1934). Basic classical commentary from the Middle Ages.

Sarna, Nahum. *Understanding Genesis* (New York: Schocken Books, 1970).

Ethics of the Fathers

Birnbaum, Philip. *The Daily Prayer Book* (New York: Hebrew Publishing Co., 1949).

Goldin, Hyman. *Ethics of the Fathers* (New York: Hebrew Publishing Co., 1962).

Goldin, Judah. *The Living Talmud* (New York: New American Library, 1957).

Herford, Travers. *The Ethics of the Talmud* (New York: Schocken Books, 1962).

Hasidim

Buber, Martin. *Tales of the Hasidim.* 2 vols. (New York: Schocken Books, 1947, 1961).

Green, Arthur, and Holtz, Barry. *Your Word is Fire: The Hasidic Masters on Contemplative Prayer* (New York: Paulist Press, 1977).

Jacobs, Louis. *Hasidic Prayer* (New York: Schocken Books, 1973).

Law and Ethics

Jacobs, Louis. *Jewish Law* (New York: Behrman House, 1968).

Maimonides

Birnbaum, Philip. *Mishneh Torah of Moses Maimonides* (New York: Hebrew Publishing Co., 1975).

Twersky, Isadore. *A Maimonides Reader* (New York: Behrman House, 1972).

Yale Judaica Series, *The Code of Maimonides* (New Haven: Yale University Press, 1956, 1961, 1965).

Stories and Folk Tales

Agnon, S.Y. *The Bridal Canopy* (New York: Schocken Books, 1967).

Agnon, S.Y. *In the Heart of the Seas* (New York: Schocken Books, 1967).

Agnon, S.Y. *Twenty-one Stories* (New York: Schocken Books, 1970).

Agnon, S.Y. *Two Tales* (New York: Schocken Books, 1966).

Ausubel, Nathan, ed. *A Treasury of Jewish Folklore* (New York: Crown Publishers, 1948).

Bin Gorion, Micha J. *Mimekor Yisrael: Classical Jewish Folktales* (Bloomington: Indiana University Press; Philadelphia: Jewish Publication Society, 1976).

Schwartz, Leo. *The Jewish Caravan* (New York: Holt, Rinehart and Winston, 1965; revised ed. New York: Schocken Books, 1976).

Cassettes and Records

Complete Friday Night Service and Songs for the Shabbat, by Cantor Abraham Davis. Noam Records NLP-105 (record and cassette).

Lekhu Neranenah, Shabbat and Hassidic Songs, by Nira Rabinowitz and Shlomo Nitzan. Vol. 1 BAN 14068; Vol. 2 BAN 14116; Vol. 3 BAN 14162 (Hed-Arzi record and cassette).

Likrat Shabbat. Prayerbook Press (cassette).

Oneg Shabbat by Serenade (record). (Includes music and words for kiddush, motzi, etc.)

Shabbat at Home. Women's League for Conservative Judaism (record).

The preceding five items are available from J. Levine Co., 58 Eldridge Street, New York, N.Y. 10002.

Shabbat Manual. Central Conference of American Rabbis. Available from CCAR, Publications Department, 790 Madison Avenue, New York, N.Y. 10021 (cassette).

Shabbat Melodies. Tara Publications and Board of Jewish Education. Available from Board of Jewish Education, 426 West 58 Street, New York, N.Y. 10019 (cassette).

Songs and Ritual for A Shabbat Haggadah, by Kenneth Cohen. Available from The American Jewish Committee, 165 East 56 Street, New York, N.Y. 10022.

souRces and acknowledgments

All copyright materials in this book have been reprinted with the permission of authors, publishers and holders of copyright. Thanks are due to:

Behrman House, Inc., for selections from *Jewish Law* by Louis Jacobs, Volume I in *The Chain of Tradition Series*, copyright 1968 by Behrman House, Inc. Reprinted by permission of the publisher.

Central Conference of American Rabbis, for the material from *Gates of the House*, copyright 1976 by Central Conference of American Rabbis of New York and the Union of Liberal and Progressive Synagogues of London, page 17.

Crown Publishers, Inc., for "Joseph della Reyna Storms Heaven" from *A Treasury of Jewish Folklore* by Nathan Ausubel, copyright 1948, 1976 by Crown Publishers, Inc.

Farrar, Straus & Giroux, Inc., for "The Jewbird" from *Idiots First* by Bernard Malamud, copyright 1963 by Bernard Malamud; for "Charity" from *In the Reign of Peace* by Hugh Nissenson, copyright 1970 by Hugh Nissenson; and for "Holiness in Time" from *The Sabbath* by Abraham Joshua Heschel, copyright 1951 by Abraham Joshua Heschel.

Arthur Green, for "Prayer of a Jewish Woman" from *The First Jewish Catalog*.

Hebrew Publishing Co., for material from *The Siddur* by Philip Birnbaum, p. xxviii and *Pirke Avot* by Philip Birnbaum, Chapter II, pp. 13–19.

Indiana University Press, for "The Generation of the Division of the Tongues" from *Mimekor Yisrael*, Volume I, pp. 24–26.

The Jewish Publication Society of America, for "The Treasure" by Isaac Leib Peretz from *Sabbath: the Day of Delight*, ed. by Abraham E. Millgram, copyright 1944, pp. 261–265; for selections from the JPS Translation of the Bible; and for "Prayer of a Jewish Woman" from *The First Jewish Catalog*.

Jonathan David Publishers, Inc., for the selection from *God, Man and History* by Eliezer Berkovits, p. 123.

Ktav Publishing House, for *Holocaust and Halakhah*, ed. by Irving Rosenbaum, pp. 25–27.

The Rabbinical Assembly, for Birkat Ha-mazon and Kiddush (long form), reprinted from the translation in *A Passover Haggadah*, copyright 1979.

Schocken Books, Inc., for "The Fable of the Goat" from *Twenty-one Stories* by S.Y. Agnon, copyright 1970, pp. 26–29.

Soncino Press Limited, for Baba Metzia 59b and Sanhedrin 68a, from *The Babylonian Talmud*, ed. by Dr. Isidor Epstein.

Tsvi Blanchard, for "The Sheep of the Hidden Valley" from *Imperial Messages*, ed. by Howard Schwartz.

The Women's League for Conservative Judaism, for the short form of Birkat Ha-mazon (translation and transliteration), copyright 1977.

124